THE
APOSTOLIC FATHERS
A New Translation and Commentary

THE APOSTOLIC FATHERS
A New Translation and Commentary
edited by Robert M. Grant
University of Chicago

Volume 1 An Introduction
  by Robert M. Grant, University of Chicago

Volume 2 First and Second Clement
  by Robert M. Grant, University of Chicago
  and Holt M. Graham, Virginia Theological Seminary

Volume 3 Barnabas and The Didache
  by Robert A. Kraft, University of Pennsylvania

Volume 4 Ignatius of Antioch
  by Robert M. Grant, University of Chicago

Volume 5 Polycarp, Martyrdom of Polycarp, Fragments of Papias
  by William R. Schoedel, Brown University

Volume 6 Hermas
  by Graydon F. Snyder, Bethany Theological Seminary

THE
APOSTOLIC FATHERS

A New Translation and Commentary

Volume 5
Polycarp, Martyrdom of Polycarp, Fragments of Papias

by
William R. Schoedel

WIPF & STOCK · Eugene, Oregon

Wipf and Stock Publishers
199 W 8th Ave, Suite 3
Eugene, OR 97401

The Apostolic Fathers, A New Translation and Commentary, Volume V
Polycarp, Martyrdom of Polycarp, Fragments of Papias
By Schoedel, William R
Copyright © 1967 by Schoedel, William R All rights reserved.
Softcover ISBN-13: 978-1-7252-8086-1
Hardcover ISBN-13: 978-1-7252-8090-8
eBook ISBN-13: 978-1-7252-8087-8
Publication date 5/18/2020
Previously published by Thomas Nelson and Sons, 1967

PREFACE

The discussion of the sources contained in this volume seeks not only to provide detailed information on special points but also to develop an interpretation of each document as a whole. In the commentary on Polycarp's letter to the Philippians this double purpose is formally reflected in a division between general observations and less connected remarks on specific terms and phrases. In the commentary on the Martyrdom of Polycarp the same division has a somewhat different significance because of the range of problems which present themselves; for some of the broader issues are most naturally explored in connection with comments on specific phrases. In the case of the fragments of Papias it was found possible—or rather necessary—to take up the discussion of details into the main line of argument. The matter of parallels to early Christian literature in the letter of Polycarp (and in the fourteenth chapter of the Martyrdom of Polycarp) required separate treatment, and the use of footnotes proved the most convenient device.

Variations in form, then, reflect in part the different nature of the sources. They also reflect, however, a search for the most economical way of presenting relevant materials. The same requirement accounts for the compressed nature of some of the commentary. As for the many parallels to which reference is made, I have always attempted to provide at least a framework in light of which they seem relevant; but limitations of space made full discussion of them impossible.

The introduction to each of the documents is intended simply to set the stage and to indicate the basic issues dealt with in the commentary. Theological concerns do not emerge in these writings as sufficiently distinct or important to warrant a summary such as that provided for Ignatius in the preceding volume of this series. The Martyrdom of Polycarp, to be sure, is an important milestone in the development of ideas concerning the martyr and can scarcely be understood in isolation; but so vast is the problem of martyrdom as a religious phenomenon that I have had to be content with making a few general suggestions in the introduction and providing materials for comparison in the commentary.

The translations have been made with one eye on the problems discussed in the commentary. At the same time I hope that they are not devoid of all literary grace. In the case of the Martyrdom of Polycarp the somewhat bloated style of the original makes a natural English version especially difficult.

I wish to take this opportunity to express thanks now long overdue to John D. Ralph of the University of Western Ontario for much by way of training and orientation which made this study possible. I am more immediately indebted to Robert M. Grant of the University of Chicago who in addition to all else has given freely of his energies in overseeing the preparation of this book. I am grateful to Otto Neugebauer of Brown University for instruction which enabled me to check the dating of Polycarp's martyrdom in so far as it depends on astronomical data.

Brown University　　　　　　　　　　　　　　William R. Schoedel
March 1967

CONTENTS

Preface   v

Abbreviations   ix

POLYCARP'S LETTER TO THE PHILIPPIANS

Introduction   3
Outline   6
Translation and Commentary   7
Selected Bibliography   42

THE MARTYRDOM OF POLYCARP

Introduction   47
Outline   50
Translation and Commentary   51
Selected Bibliography   83

THE FRAGMENTS OF PAPIAS

Introduction   89
Outline   93
Translation and Commentary   94
The Traditions of the Elders   124
Selected Bibliography   128

ABBREVIATIONS

1. The writings of the Apostolic Fathers:

Barn.	Epistle of Barnabas
1 Clem.	Clement of Rome to the Corinthians
2 Clem.	2 Clement (sermon)
Did.	The Didache
Diog.	Epistle to Diognetus
Ign. Eph.	Ignatius to the Ephesians
Ign. Magn.	Ignatius to the Magnesians
Ign. Philad.	Ignatius to the Philadelphians
Ign. Polyc.	Ignatius to Polycarp
Ign. Rom.	Ignatius to the Romans
Ign. Smyrn.	Ignatius to the Smyrnaeans
Ign. Trall.	Ignatius to the Trallians
Mand.	Hermas, Mandates
Mart. Polyc.	Martyrdom of Polycarp
Polyc. Phil.	Polycarp to the Philippians
Sim.	Hermas, Similitudes
Vis.	Hermas, Visions

2. Other writers and writings of antiquity (abbreviations infrequently used yet reasonably clear are omitted here):

Ad Autol.	Theophilus, *Ad Autolycum*
Adv. haer.	Irenaeus, *Adversus haereses*
Anaph. Serap.	*The Anaphora of Serapion of Thmuis*
Ann.	Tacitus, *Annales*
Ant.	Josephus, *Antiquitates*
Apol.	Justin, *Apology;* Plato, *Apology*
ApCo	Apostolic Constitutions
Bell.	Josephus, *Bellum Iudaicum*
De Fabr. Mund.	Victorinus, *De Fabricia Mundi*
Dial.	Justin, *Dialogue with Trypho*
Dig.	*Digesta*

Dio	Dio Cassius
D.L.	Diogenes Laertius
Ep.	*Epistles* (by various authors)
Exc. ex Theod.	Clement, *Excerpta ex Theodoto*
G. Thomas	The Coptic Gospel of Thomas
H.E.	Eusebius, *Historia Ecclesiastica*
Inst.	Quintilian, *Institutiones Oratoriae*
Jub.	Book of Jubilees
Leg.	Athenagoras, *Legatio*
Mart. Apoll.	Martyrdom of Apollonius
Mart. Carp.	Martyrdom of Carpus
Mart. Iren.	Martyrdom of Irenaeus
Mart. Isa.	Martyrdom of Isaiah
Mart. Just.	Martyrdom of Justin
Mart. Perp.	Martyrdom of Perpetua
Mart. Pion.	Martyrdom of Pionius
Mart. Polyc.	Martyrdom of Polycarp
Mem.	Xenophon, *Memorabilia*
M.P.	Eusebius, *Martyrs of Palestine*
Nat. hist.	Pliny, *Naturalis historia*
Paed.	Clement, *Paedagogus*
Ref.	Hippolytus, *Refutation of All Heresies*
Sir.	Sirach
Str.	Clement, *Stromata*
T. Jud.	*Testaments of the Twelve Patriarchs: Testament of Jude*
Vit. Apollon.	Philostratus, *Vita Apollonii*

3. Periodicals, encyclopedias, collections, dictionaries:

AB	*Analecta Bollandiana*
ACW	*Ancient Christian Writers*, ed. J. Quasten and J. C. Plumpe
AkGWG	*Abhandlungen der königlichen Gesellschaft der Wissenschaften zu Göttingen: Philologisch-historische Klasse*
ATR	*Anglican Theological Review*

ABBREVIATIONS

BAG	Walter Bauer, *A Greek-English Lexicon of the New Testament*, trans. W. F. Arndt and F. W. Gingrich (Chicago, 1957)
B-D	F. Blass and A. Debrunner, *A Greek Grammar of the New Testament*, trans. R. W. Funk (Chicago, 1961)
BZ	*Biblische Zeitschrift*
CIG (Boeckh)	*Corpus Inscriptionum Graecarum*, ed. A. Boeckh (Berlin, 1828-1877)
CIL	*Corpus Inscriptionum Latinarum*
DCG	*Dictionary of Christ and the Gospels*, ed. J. Hastings
GIF	*Giornale Italiano di Filologia*
HTR	*Harvard Theological Review*
HZ	*Historische Zeitschrift*
IG	*Inscriptiones Graecae*
JQR	*Jewish Quarterly Review*
JTS	*Journal of Theological Studies*
LSJ	H. G. Liddell and R. Scott, *A Greek-English Lexicon*, 9th ed. rev. H. S. Jones (Oxford, 1940)
PB	*Pastor Bonus*
PG	*Patrologiae Cursus Completus: Series Graeca*, ed. J.-P. Migne
PWK	*Paulys Realencyclopädie der classischen Altertumswissenschaft*, ed. G. Wissowa and W. Kroll
RGG	*Die Religion in Geschichte und Gegenwart*
RQ	*Römische Quartalschrift*
SHA	*Sitzungsberichte der Heidelberger Akademie der Wissenschaften: Philosophische-historische Klasse*
SJT	*Scottish Journal of Theology*
ThS	*Theological Studies*
ThZ	*Theologische Zeitschrift*
TU	*Texte und Untersuchungen*
VC	*Vigiliae Christianae*

| ZNW | *Zeitschrift für die neutestamentliche Wissenschaft* |
| ZWT | *Zeitschrift für wissenschafliche Theologie* |

4. Miscellaneous:

Cod.	Codex
exc.	excerpt
inscr.	Inscription (salutation)
LXX	Septuagint
praef.	*praefatio* (preface)
prol.	prologue

THE
APOSTOLIC FATHERS
A New Translation and Commentary

POLYCARP'S LETTER TO THE PHILIPPIANS

POLYCARP'S LETTER TO THE PHILIPPIANS

Introduction

Polycarp was regarded by Irenaeus and after him Eusebius not only as a peacemaker in the Church (Eusebius, *H.E.* 5.24.14-18) but also as an important link in a significant chain of anti-Gnostic tradition stretching from the apostles to the catholic church of the latter part of the second century (Irenaeus, *Adv. haer.* 3.3.4; Eusebius, *H.E.* 3.36.1,10; 4.14.1-9; 5.20.4-8). Modern scholars are skeptical of these claims; and it is likely that especially the idea of a close connection between Polycarp and the apostle John (Irenaeus in Eusebius, *H.E.* 5.20.6; Tertullian, *De Praescriptione* 32) rests on a misunderstanding (A. H. McNeile, *An Introduction to the Study of the New Testament* [rev. ed., Oxford, 1953], 282-284). Yet there is little doubt that it was through men like Polycarp that the foundations of the catholic church were laid. His teaching echoes an important side of the apostolic witness; and the evidence which points to the relative respectability of Gnosticism within the Church in this period has (as we shall see) been exaggerated (see pp. 7-8, 12, 100).

We know what we do about Polycarp from the passages in Eusebius noted above, from Ignatius' letters (especially to Smyrna and Polycarp), from the Martyrdom of Polycarp, and from the letter of Polycarp to the Philippians. According to Irenaeus, Polycarp wrote "letters . . . to the neighboring churches, confirming them, [and] to some of the brethren, admonishing and exhorting them" (Eusebius, *H.E.* 5.20.8). But he seems actually to have known only the letter to the Philippians: "Now there is also a letter of Polycarp written to the Philippians, a most adequate one; from which such as so desire, and have a care for their own salvation, can learn both the character of his faith and the message of the truth" (Irenaeus *Adv. haer.* 3.3.4; Eusebius, *H.E.* 4.14.8). Of the fragments attributed to Polycarp, none seems worthy of attention (Meinhold, PWK, XXI, 1689-1691).

The authenticity of the letter to the Philippians was at one time questioned by those seeking to discredit an early witness to Ignatius' letters (cf. Polyc. Phil. 13). Lightfoot and Zahn succeeded in showing to the satisfaction of most that the letters of both Ignatius (uninterpolated) and Polycarp accorded well with what could be known of the early second century. As for the numerous theories of interpolation, these are, as Voelter pp. 16-28 has shown, unconvincing. His own theory (pp. 19-28), however, is worth mention. He eliminates all reference to Ignatius: "that you received . . . chosen by God and our Lord and" (1:1), "Ignatius and" (9:1), and the whole of chapter 13. His arguments, however, are tenuous (the lack of grammatical symmetry in 1:1; the failure of Ignatius to refer to the companions mentioned in 9:1). (See also p. 39.) More convincing is the thesis of P. N. Harrison that we have here two letters of Polycarp (chs. 1–12; 13–14). Harrison's work sheds much light on the epistle, but I have come to the conclusion that even this theory is unnecessary (see pp. 29, 37). I hope to convince the student of Polycarp that despite the simplicity of the man's thought and the directness of his expression, the major issues raised by the situation which he confronted are carefully interwoven with one another and to a degree appropriately related to the traditional material he adopts; and I shall try to show that not only is there no decisive argument against accepting the letter in its present form but also that our analysis of the argument favors a conservative estimate of the literary problem. I count particularly P. Meinhold (PWK, XXI, 1662-1693) as a predecessor in the effort to uncover the inner coherence of Polycarp's letter; if I disagree with his analysis (and consequently also his evaluation of Harrison's thesis), it is not out of any disrespect for his work from which I have learned much.

The date of Polycarp's letter can be determined, then, only by reference to Ignatius. The latter's martyrdom took place, according to Eusebius (in the *Chronicon*), in the eleventh year of Trajan (A.D. 108). This date is under a cloud, but few seem disposed to challenge the suggestion that it was within Trajan's reign (A.D. 98–117) that Ignatius was martyred.

Our translation seeks to show by means of italics Polycarp's deep indebtedness to biblical and early Christian sources. There are many different ways in which such language may have come to form part of his vocabulary. Only where I was fairly certain that Polycarp reflects more or less direct contact with the texts involved have I made use of quotation marks. By this criterion the following books may be listed as attested to: Psalms, Proverbs, Isaiah, Jeremiah, Ezekiel, Tobit; Matthew, Luke, Acts, Romans, 1-2 Corinthians, Galatians, Ephesians, Philippians, 1-2 Timothy, 1 Peter, 1 John; 1 Clement. The use of the Old Testament is slight; the case of Acts (p. 8) and that of 1 John (p. 24) are perhaps doubtful; Polycarp seems to have been particularly familiar with 1 Clement. There is no evidence that any of the New Testament books are regarded as Scripture.

Von Campenhausen (*SHA*, 1951, No. 2) has argued that Polycarp wrote the Pastorals and that consequently it is inaccurate to speak of quotations from these writings in our letter (see p. 16). He points to the difference in purpose to account for the (relatively superficial?) ways in which Polycarp to the Philippians and the Pastorals diverge; beyond that the similarity in historical setting, style, and thought must be granted. It is my feeling that it is almost impossible to prove or disprove this theory in any conclusive way. We may suggest, however, for whatever it is worth, that there is at least in one area a difference which cannot be accounted for in the way indicated: the Pastorals make an unusual use of categories linked with the cult of the emperor in their Christology (*sōtēr, epiphaneia;* cf. Dibelius pp. 74-78); these we may fairly have expected to be echoed in Polycarp to the Philippians if the author were in fact the same. We may also note that in another important case the similarity is uncertain (see p. 7).

There are nine Greek manuscripts of the letter, four of which also contain the interpolated letters of Ignatius. All come from a common source since they all end with the words *kai di' hēmas hypo* in 9:2, which is immediately followed by *ton laon ton kainon*, etc., of Barnabas 5:7. The best of them is Codex Vaticanus Graecus 859 (eleventh century). There is a Latin version from which the rest of the letter is translated. Eusebius (*H.E.* 3.36.13-15), however, supplies us with the Greek for the whole of chapter 9 and for chapter 13 (though he does not give us the crucial last line). We have made use particularly of the text of Karl Bihlmeyer, *Die apostolischen Vaeter: Neubearbeitung der Funkschen Ausgabe,* rev. Wilhelm Schneemelcher, I (Tübingen: J. C. B. Mohr [Paul Siebeck], 1956), 114-120.

Outline

Salutation (Inscription)
I. Grounds for rejoicing (1:1-3)
II. Service to God (2:1-3)
III. Righteousness according to Paul (3:1-3)
IV. Table of duties I (4:1-3)
V. Table of duties II (5:1–6:3)
VI. Docetism (7:1-2)
VII. The imitation of Christ (8:1-2)
VIII. The martyrs (9:1-2)
IX. The brotherhood (10:1-3)
X. Love of money: Valens (11:1-4a)
XI. Sobriety "in this thing" (11:4b–12:1)
XII. The prayer (12:2-3)
XIII. The letters of Ignatius (13:1-2)
XIV. Conclusion (14:1)

Polycarp to the Philippians

Translation[1] and Commentary

Salutation (Inscription)
Polycarp *and the elders with him,*[2] *"to the church of God sojourning at* Philippi";[3] *mercy "and peace be multiplied to you*[4] *from God almighty and Jesus Christ"*[3] *our savior.*[5]

[1] Quotations and allusions: Words and phrases reflecting the language of the Bible and early Chrisitan literature before the time of Polycarp are italicized. Where more or less clear contact with the actual text seems presupposed, quotation marks are used.
[2] Ign. Philad. inscr.
[3] 1 Clem. inscr. (cf. 1 Tim. 1:2; 2 Tim. 1:2).
[4] Jude 2; cf. 2 Pet. 1:2.
[5] Tit. 1:4.

Salutation. This subapostolic form of greeting betrays the influence both of Pauline and Jewish models. For the latter see the form of address in 2 Baruch 78:2 ("Mercy and peace") and the blessing in Tobit 7:12 (S) (cf. Gal. 6:16).
Polycarp: Employed as an adjective ("fruitful") since Homer. This appears to be the first instance in Greek sources of its use as a proper noun; but Greek inscriptions from the second century know the name (*IG*, II, 2142?; *IG*, III, 1122, 1163, 1171, 1193, 1259; *IG*, IX/2, 25a; L. and J. Robert, *La Carie* [Paris, 1954], II, 119) and it is found already in Latin inscriptions from Pompeii (*CIL*, IV, 2351, 2470). Polycarp does not refer to himself as a "bishop" though there can be no doubt that he was (Ign. Magn. 15; Smyrn. 12:2; Polyc. inscr.; Mart. Polyc. 16:2). The bishop, however, was closely connected with the elders (see n. 2) and was regarded in certain early and late second-century sources as a *primus inter pares*—a "fellow elder" (1 Pet. 5:1; Tit. 1:5-9; Eusebius, *H.E.* 5.24.14; 5.16.5). This may explain Polycarp's reticence. Zahn (*Ignatius*, 296-301), however, insists that there is no difference between Polycarp and Ignatius on this point. He notes that neither does Igantius refer to himself as "bishop" in his salutations and that the absence of a reference to a "bishop" elsewhere in Polycarp's letter could well reflect the fact that there was no monarchical bishop in Philippi (there may still have been many "bishops"—cf. Phil. 1:1). *The elders with him:* Bauer (*Rechtgläubigkeit*, 74) has argued that this phrase has to do with the elders who are on

I. Grounds for rejoicing (1:1-3)

1 *I rejoice with you greatly in our Lord Jesus Christ* [1] that you received the images of true love and helped on their way, as was your part, those confined in *holy* [2] *bonds*,[3] which are *diadems* [4] for *them who are truly chosen by God and our Lord;* [5] 2. and (I rejoice) that the *firm* [6] *root* [7] of your *faith*,[6] *proclaimed* [8] *from earliest times*,[9] perdures until now and *bears fruit unto* [10] our Lord Jesus Christ, *who endured* [11] to face even death *for our sins*,[12] *"whom God raised having loosed the pangs of Hades";* [13]

[1] Phil. 4:10; 2:17. [2] 1 Clem. 13:3 (*hagioprepēs*).
[3] Ign. Smyrn. 11:1 ("most godly bonds").
[4] Rev. 19:12 (cf. Ign. Eph. 11:2).
[5] 1 Clem. 50:7. [6] 1 Clem. 1:2; 6:2.
[7] Luke 8:13 (see n. 10). [8] Rom. 1:8.
[9] Acts 15:7, 21 (cf. Phil. 4:15).
[10] Mt. 13:23; Luke 8:15; Rom. 7:4; Col. 1:6.
[11] Heb. 12:2. [12] 1 Cor. 15:3.
[13] Acts 2:24. The juxtaposition of Acts 2:24 and 1 Pet. 1:8 may be significant since the first is drawn from a sermon of Peter. If Polycarp is consciously bringing "Petrine" material together, it greatly increases the likelihood that he knew the book of Acts. At any rate, there seems to be no way of proving that the parallel to Acts is a variant of "an old kerygmatic formula" (E. Haenchen, *Apostelgeschichte* [Göttingen, 1959], 5). The reading "Hades" (D Lat Cop-bo Syr-vg Irenaeus) instead of "death" may, however, presuppose an exegetical tradition. The expression "pangs of death" occurs in Ps. 18:4 (cf. Ps. 116:3) LXX; the expression "pangs of Hades" begins the following verse. This passage may have been discovered because of its proximity to Ps. 16:8-11 quoted in Acts 2:25-28. It is likely that the appearance of "Hades" also in Acts 2:27 (Ps. 16:10) contributed to the development. (Job 39:2 provides only a verbal parallel to our passage.)

Polycarp's side (against those adhering to Docetic views). This is incorrect. The construction (cf. especially Gal. 1:1-2) underscores the close relationship between Polycarp and the elders at Smyrna. An opposition is not necessarily implied. *Sojourning:* For the biblical roots of this idea see 1 Peter 2:11 (Ps. 39:12; cf. Gen. 23:4; Lev. 25:23; 1 Chron. 29:15; Heb. 11:13). The term is modified somewhat by the Jewish conception of the Dispersion (Sir. prol.; cf. Jas. 1:1; 1 Pet. 1:1). In Philo (*De Confusione Linguarum* 80-81) it is interpreted within the framework of a Stoic-Platonic scheme and refers to the wise man's exile in a material body. Presumably Polycarp and 1 Clement are closer to 1 Peter, where the theme is related to ideas of God's election, his foreknowledge, and his redemptive activity in the end time (1 Pet. 1:1-2; 17-21). But see Martyrdom of Polycarp, inscription.

1:1-3. Polycarp begins by mentioning two reasons for his rejoicing

3. *"in whom without having seen you believe with unutterable and exalted joy,"* [14] *into which many desire to enter,* [15] *knowing that* [16] *"by grace you have been saved," "not of works,"* [17] *but by the will of God* [18] *through Jesus Christ.* [19]

[14] 1 Pet. 1:8.
[15] Structurally an adaptation of 1 Pet. 1:12; but the content is reminiscent of Matt. 25:21, 23.
[16] Rom. 5:3; 2 Cor. 1:7; 3:2; Phil. 1:16; 1 Pet. 1:18, etc. See also on 4:1; 5:1; and 6:1.
[17] Eph. 2:5, 8, 9.   [18] Eph. 1:5, 9, 11.
[19] Eph. 1:5.

---

with the Philippians: (1) they received Ignatius and his companions on their way to martyrdom in Rome (vs. 1; cf. 9:1; 13:2) and (2) their ancient faith remains and brings forth fruit unto Christ (vs. 2a). Appended to this is a long series of subordinate clauses describing the redemptive activity of Christ (vss. 2b-3).

Information about Ignatius and his companions (vs. 1; cf. 9:1) may well have been contained in the same letter from the Philippians referred to elsewhere (3:1); see further on 13:1-2. The opening lines of the letter presuppose a fresh memory of the martyrs and do not allow for a lapse of some twenty years, as proposed by Harrison pp. 155-162, between the departure of Ignatius from Philippi and this section of Polycarp's letter (H. C. Puech, *Revue de l'histoire des religions*, 119 [1939], 102). Even if we were to accept Harrison's theory, then, and divide the letter into two (chs. 13-14 and chs.1-12), the second would have followed soon upon the first (C. J. Cadoux, *JTS*, 38 [1937], 268; see now L. W. Barnard, *Church Quarterly Review*, 163 [1962], 421-430).

The references to the martyrs in the letter (vs. 1; 9:1; 13:2) indicate the importance of the theme to Polycarp. This is possibly rooted in the fact that the recognition of Ignatius was a blow against teachers of Docetism (7:1). The two reasons for rejoicing (vss. 1-2), then, are related: *recognition of the martyrs is a manifestation of the ancient orthodox faith of Philippi.*

The emphasis on the death and resurrection of Christ (vss. 2-3) may be similarly motivated. The stress on the resurrection is especially strong in the letter, and we shall see that it is indirectly connected with an anti-Docetic note already in 2:1. The theme of salvation by grace without works (1:3) presupposes a "faith" which "bears fruit" (1:2; see n. 10; cf. Philo, *De Cherubim* 84-85) and finds a place side by side with Polycarp's rather vigorous "moralism" (2:2-3). It is likely, as we shall see, that the work of Christ is understood by Polycarp as providing the basis for the forgiveness of sins (6:2) apprehended through "repentance" (11:4). The Christian's new obedience amounts to a renewed striving on the basis of natural powers once the burden of past sin has been lifted. It is not rooted in a fundamentally trans-

II. Service to God (2:1-3)

2 *"Therefore gird up your loins"* [1] and *serve God in fear and truth;* [2] *give up empty, vain discussion* [3] and the *error* [4] of the crowd; believe "him *who raised* our Lord Jesus Christ *from the dead and gave him glory"* [5] and a *throne* [6] *at his right hand,* [7] to whom were *subjected all things* [8] *in heaven and earth,* [9] whom *every breathing thing* [10] serves, who *is coming* [11] as *judge of the*

[1] 1 Pet. 1:13.
[2] Ps. 2:11; Tob. 14:9 (S); Eph. 6:14; 1 Clem. 19:1.
[3] 1 Clem. 7:2; 9:1; 1 Tim. 1:6 (*mataiologia*).
[4] Eph. 4:14; 1 John 4:6 (cf. 2 John 7).
[5] 1 Pet. 1:21.   [6] 1 Clem. 65:2 (cf. Sir. 47:11).
[7] Cf. Ps. 110:1, cited frequently in NT.
[8] Phil. 3:21; 1 Cor. 15:26-27.   [9] Phil. 2:10.
[10] 1 Kings 15:29; Ps. 150:6; Isa. 57:16.
[11] Acts 1:11; Matt. 25:31.

---

formed existence. Note the absence of eschatological intensity and the lack of interest in the "Spirit" of God. The resurrection of the believer, the possibility of which was demonstrated in Christ and which is acknowledged by "faith," is contingent upon uprightness and the exercise of brotherly love (2:2; 5:2).

1:1. *Images of true love:* Literally "images of the true love." Possibly "the True Love" is Christ (cf. John 14:6; 1 John 4:8-10). But nowhere is Christ explicitly called "love" as he is called "the truth." It is better to understand the phrase as referring to love which reaches out for men, which was manifested in Christ, and which is imitated by his followers (cf. Mart. Polyc. 1:2). *Images:* For the theme of the imitation of Christ's sufferings see 8:2; Ign. Romans 6:3 (cf. 4 Macc. 9:23; 13:9). The Hermetic parallel (*Corpus Hermeticum, Exc.* IIA, 4) is purely verbal. *Diadems:* The word also means "crowns"; but the use of the plural suggests that the reference is to the band worn in the first instance by the Persian king (Xenophon, *Cyropaedia* 8.3.13) and later by Greek kings generally (Plutarch, *Amatorius* 753d). In Polycarp the phrase as a whole seems to be modeled on Ignatius, Smyrnaeans 11:1 ("most godly bonds") and Ephesians 11:2 ("bonds" as "spiritual pearls"). The image of the diadem or crown may well have been traditional in such a setting (cf. 4 Macc. 17:12, 15; Rev. 19:12; Mart. Polyc. 17:1). It need not be the result of years of reflection (Harrison p. 160). In any event, the remark has all the appearance of a reply to a recent communication. The epistolary aorist (*synecharēn*) in particular functions as does the "contristatus sum" (*synelypēthēn?*) in 11:1 to introduce a topic broached by the Philippians. (For similar metaphors see Eusebius, *H.E.* 5.1.35; Cyprian, *Ep.* 76.2.)

2.1-3. *Therefore . . . serve God.* Such service involves (1) avoid-

living and the dead,¹² whose *blood God will require* ¹³ *of those who disobey* ¹⁴ *him*. 2. And *"he who raised him"* ¹⁵ *from the dead* ¹⁶ *"will also raise us"* ¹⁵ if *we do his will* ¹⁷ and *walk in his commandments* ¹⁸ and love the things he loved, *abstaining*

---

¹² Acts 10:42 (probably a conventional formula; cf. 1 Pet. 4:5; 2 Tim. 4:1).
¹³ Gen. 42:22; 2 Sam. 4:11; Ezek. 3:18, 20; 33:6, 8; Luke 11:50, 51.
¹⁴ 1 Pet. 4:17; Rom. 15:31.
¹⁵ 2 Cor. 4:14 (cf. 1 Cor. 6:14; Ign. Trall. 9:2).
¹⁶ Rom. 8:11.   ¹⁷ Heb. 10:36; 13:21; 1 John 2:17.
¹⁸ Luke 1:6.

---

ing heretics ("the vain discussion . . . of the crowd" is to be connected with 7:2, where the same term occurs) and (2) believing in him who raised and exalted Christ. The possibility also of the believer's resurrection is thus demonstrated; but it is contingent on doing the will of God which includes (*a*) the avoidance of vices and (*b*) the willingness to suffer for righteousness' sake in showing mercy to others.

The emphasis on resurrection probably means that rejection of it was an element in the error to which Polycarp refers (vs. 1; cf. 7:1). Polycarp's emphasis on judgment (vs. 1) and his teaching that resurrection is contingent on doing God's will (vs. 2) suggest that both were also denied by the errorists (7:1; cf. Ireanaeus, *Adv. haer.* 1.6.1-4).

The emphasis on showing mercy and forgiveness (2:3) may have further ramifications since it is related to similar themes in 6:2; 11:4; 12:1. Polycarp may be anticipating the discussion concerning Valens and his wife. Heretics are to be avoided, but erring brethren shown mercy. Note also the first warning against "love of money" (vs. 2), which was Valens' failing (11:1). It is not impossible that 1 Peter 3:9 and Matthew 5:3, 10, whatever their original meaning, were also felt by Polycarp to apply to disturbances which the situation described in 11:1–12:1 had caused. Matthew 5:10 also prepares the way for the discussion of "righteousness" in the next paragraph.

2:1. *Vain discussion, error:* Vanity and error in Jewish and Christian sources refer particularly to (*a*) the idolatry or worldliness of the pagans (vanity: Wisd. 13:1; Acts 14:15; 1 Cor. 3:20; 1 Pet. 1:18; Barn. 4:10; Hermas, Mand. 11:8; error: 2 Thess. 2:11; Barn. 4:1; 14:5; Ign. Eph. 10:2; vanity and error: Rom. 1:21, 27; Eph. 4:14, 17) and to (*b*) the errors and vices of heretics (vanity: Tit. 3:9; Ign. Philad. 1:1?; error: 2 Pet. 3:17; Jude 11; 1 John 4:6; vanity and error: 2 Pet. 2:18). *Vain discussion* is used of heresy in 1 Timothy 1:6 (cf. Tit. 1:10); the term occurs only here and in Polycarp within the NT and the Apostolic Fathers. (The "verbosity" and "vain discussion" of *Corp. Herm.* 14:4 has to do with wrong philosophical opin-

from [19] all unrighteousness,[20] greed,[21] love of money,[22] evil speech,[23] false witness; [24] "not returning evil for evil or abuse for abuse" [25] or blow for blow or curse for curse; 3. but remembering what the Lord said as he taught: [26] "Judge not that you be not judged"; [27] "forgive and you will be forgiven"; [26] "have mercy that you may receive mercy"; [26] "the measure you give will be the measure you get back"; [28] and "blessed are the poor and those who are persecuted for righteousness' sake, for theirs is the kingdom of God." [29]

[19] Job 2:3 (1:1, 8); 1 Thess. 5:22; 1 Pet. 2:11.   [20] Rom. 1:29.
[21] Rom. 1:29.   [22] 1 Tim. 6:10; 3:3; 2 Tim. 3:2; Heb. 13:5.
[23] 1 Pet. 2:1.   [24] Matt. 15:19.   [25] 1 Pet. 3:9.
[26] 1 Clem. 13:1-2 (cf. Acts 20:35).
[27] Matt. 7:1.
[28] 1 Clem. 13:2; Matt. 7:2; Luke 6:38 (". . . get back").
[29] Matt. 5:3 with Matt. 5:10; cf. Luke 6:20 (". . . kingdom of God"). The basis of the whole of 2:3 is 1 Clem. 13:1-2; but it was apparently cited by memory and shows the influence of the synoptic tradition in details. That especially Matthew was before Polycarp in written form is proved by the peculiarly Matthean elements in the final quotation (the variations which approach the Lucan tradition may show the influence also of that Gospel or may be the marks of quoting from memory). See Koester pp. 4–6, 112, 115–118.

---

ions.) In Polycarp the reference appears to be to the errors and vices of heretics (cf. 7:2). *Crowd* (cf. 7:2): Literally "the many." Bauer (*Rechtgläubigkeit*, 76-77) has argued that this is proof of the preponderance of Docetists in Smyrna. "The many" is a statistical concept (2 Macc. 2:27; Josephus, *Ant.* 3.212; Eusebius, *H.E.* 2.2.2) but most often also has a pejorative connotation (Philo, *Heres* 42; Epictetus, *Discourses* 1.2.18; 1.3.4; Plotinus, *Enneads* 2.9.9; Eusebius, *H.E.* 3.39.3; 4.23.7). It is artificial here to press the statistical side. The evidence brought forward above suggests that the vanity and error of heresy was not felt to be radically distinct from that of (numerically superior) paganism. Note that the heretical "vain speakers" of Titus 1:10 are condemned for lying *as Cretans* from the mouth of a pagan poet. 2:2. *Love of money:* The list of vices in which this term occurs is reminiscent particularly of 1 Clement 35:5. There, however, love of money does not appear. Despite its subordinate place in our list, it is of central importance in the letter as a whole as we shall see. *Blow, curse:* The term *gronthos* ("blow") is rare; it was regarded by the Atticists as improper (BAG, 166). It occurs in Aquila's version of Exodus 21:18, which is near "an eye for an eye, and a tooth for a tooth" (21:24). Since we are here dealing with the evangelic correction of that principle, Harrison p. 171 conjectures that the term is an echo of Aquila's version. This would support a later date for this part

III. Righteousness according to Paul (3:1-3)

3 *I write these things to you,[1] brethren,[2] concerning righteousness [3] not on my own initiative but because you first invited me. 2. For neither I nor any other like me can attain the wisdom of the*

[1] 1 Cor. 4:14; 2 Cor. 13:10; 1 Tim. 3:14.
[2] Rom. 1:13, etc.
[3] Acts 24:25.

---

of the letter. All that, however, is very tenuous. It is more likely that the thought was derived from Matthew 5:39 (or, better perhaps, Luke 6:29, since Luke 6:28 also bids us to bless those who "curse" us), the form from the preceding quotation, and the term *gronthos* from daily speech.

3.1–3. Polycarp responds to the Philippians' request (no doubt communicated to him by letter) to discuss the meaning of the (Pauline) term righteousness (vs. 1). The response consists of (1) an expression of admiration for Paul's wisdom (vs. 2) and (2) a brief exegesis based on the Pauline "faith, hope, and love" and the two great commandments of the Gospels (vs. 3).

The *tauta* with which this paragraph beings makes it clear that *what precedes is regarded as the substance of "righteousness."* There seems to be a twofold connection between the second and third chapters: (1) Paul in particular has been appealed to by false teachers (probably those referred to in 2:1), and his doctrine of righteousness has been misrepresented. We may assume that righteousness was the actual term under investigation since Polycarp is so careful to define it and since it recurs so often in the epistle (vss. 1, 3; 2:3; 4:1; 5:2; 8:1; 9:1, 2). Polycarp's humility before the wisdom of Paul (vs. 2) can be understood only as including a warning against a facile treatment of the difficult doctrine of righteousness by grace without the works of the law (cf. 1:3). (2) At the same time, vss. 1-3 have a connection with 2:2–3. Polycarp keeps in mind the problems hinted at there; hence the interpretation of righteousness as "love" and the concern in 4:1 ff. for the fulfillment of duties. We shall see later how the two issues—heresy and Valens' love of money—interpenetrate.

It is impossible to tell exactly what the errorists taught about "righteousness." Meinhold (PWK, XXI, 1685) has suggested that it is the Marcionite speculation. Marcion not only devaluated the righteousness of the creator but also knew of a higher righteousness (Harnack pp. 111-113). Similar speculation is also known among the Valentinians (Harnack p. 112 n. 2, who thinks it dependent on Marcion; cf. Ptolemaeus, *Letter to Flora* 5; Clement, *Exc. ex Theod.* 37). An earlier libertine interpretation of basic Pauline categories (in Eph. 2:8-9) is known to us from Irenaeus' account of the teaching of Simon Magus (*Adv. haer.* 1.23.3).

It is also of interest to note that Ptolemaeus used the story of the rich young man (Matt. 19:16-22) to show that (psychic) righteous-

blessed and glorious Paul,[4] who, when he was among you *face to face* [5] with the men of that day, *taught accurately* [6] and authoritatively *the word of truth* [7] and who, *when he was absent*,[8] wrote you *letters*,[8] *through the study* [9] of which *you will be able* [10] to be

[4] Cf. 2 Pet. 3:15.   [5] 2 Cor. 10:1.   [6] Acts 18:25.
[7] Col. 1:5 (cf. 1:4-5: faith, love, hope); 2 Cor 6:6 (love also mentioned here; 6:7 quoted by Polycarp in the next chapter).
[8] 2 Cor. 10:1, 11 (Phil. 1:27).
[9] 1 Clem. 45:2 (*egkekyphate*).   [10] Eph. 3:4.

ness is distinct from (spiritual) perfection (Irenaeus, *Adv. haer.* 1.8.3). The requirements of the law were observed by the young man; yet he was not perfect. Now in Matthew 19:19 the command to love the neighbor is among these requirements. It is tempting to think that such an exegesis was known to Polycarp and that he sought to undercut it by linking the Matthean demands of righteousness with the (presumably higher) Pauline way of righteousness by means of the command to love the neighbor (see nn. 12, 14, 16, 17).

3:1. *First invited me:* Read *proepekalesasthe* (Lightfoot, Funk, Bihlmeyer). There is no more lexical support for this conjecture than Zahn's *proepelaktisasthe;* but it appears more within the range of possibilities and is supported by the Latin translation (*provocastis*).
3:2. *Blessed:* Of Paul also in 11:3; 1 Clement 47:1; of Ignatius and others in 9:1; of Polycarp in Martyrdom of Polycarp 1:1; 19:1; 21; 22; Eusebius, *H.E.* 5.20.6-7. Not necessarily of the dead in our period but more and more tending in that direction (Delehaye, *Sanctus*, 59-72). It has a special connection with martyrs (cf. Origen, *Exhortation to Martyrdom* 31) and serves as a predecessor to the term "saint." Its significance in Greek theology comes to fullest expression in Gregory of Nyssa (*PG*, XLIV, 433c): God alone is blessed "in his nature"; the term may be used of men only by reason of their "participation in True Being." *Letters:* In the Classical period the plural of the word often referred to a single letter (so also Eusebius, *H.E.* 6.43.3); but in literature contemporary with Polycarp it seems to be a true plural (BAG, 300). The following suggestions have been made: (*a*) Polycarp actually knew of more than one letter to the Philippians (note the double reference to a letter "of the Philippians" in a Syriac canon from *ca.* A.D. 400; but it seems to be a textual error; cf. A. Souter, *The Text and Canon of the New Testament*, rev. C. S. C. Williams [London, 1954], 209). (*b*) Our present Philippians is a composite of letters to Philippi, the parts of which were known to Polycarp in separated form. (*c*) Polycarp deduced the existence of more than one letter from Paul (Phil. 3:1). (*d*) Polycarp had in mind Philippians and 1-2 Thessalonians, since the Macedonian congregations were looked upon as a unit (2 Cor. 8:1-2; cf. Zahn, *Introduction*, I, 536). (*e*) Ed. Schweizer (*ThZ*, 1 [1945], 90-105) has suggested that 2 Thessalonians was originally a letter to the Philippians (see on 11:3

built up in [11] *the "faith"* [12] *given you* 3. *"which is the mother of us all"* [13]—*"hope"* [12] *following after, and "love"* [12] *toward God and Christ and toward the neighbor* [14] *going on ahead; for if a man be in this company,* [15] *he has fulfilled* [16] *the commandment* [14] *of righteousness;* [17] *for he who has love* [18] *is far* [19] *from all sin.* [20]

[11] 1 Cor. 8:10.
[12] 1 Cor. 13:13; 1 Thess. 1:3; see n. 7.
[13] Gal. 4:26 speaks of the heavenly Jerusalem "which is the mother of us." "Of us all" is read not only by Polycarp but also by A Byz Syr-h Irenaeus Origen. This reading may arise from a rhetorical impulse or an exegetical tradition involving Rom. 4:16-17 and Gal. 4:22-26 (J. C. Plumpe, *Mater Ecclesia* [Washington, 1943], 18–19). Abraham, the "father of us all," is originator of Christians through Sarah—that is, faith—who is, therefore, the mother of us all. For other early references to faith as mother (in much different settings) see Hermas, Vis. 3.8.5; Mart. Just. 4.8.
[14] Matt. 22:36-40.   [15] Ign. Eph. 5:2.
[16] Rom. 13:8, 10 (Gal. 5:14).   [17] Matt. 3:15.
[18] 1 Cor. 13:1; 1 Clem. 49:1.
[19] Sir. 15:8; Ep. Jer. 72.
[20] 1 John 1:7; 3:9-11; cf. 2:29 ("righteousness" an ethical category).

---

below). It seems more likely that we have here no more than an imprecision arising from familiarity with Pauline phraseology: The antithesis between "when he was absent" and "face to face" occurs in 2 Corinthians 10:1; soon thereafter (10:11) Paul speaks of his influence "through letters when he was absent"; the same "when he was absent" also occurs in Philippians 1:27. 3:2–3. *Faith, hope, love:* Three interpretations are possible: (a) Hope follows faith; love precedes it (for *proagein* of temporal precedence see BAG, 709); the order love, faith, hope is found in Clement, *Quis Dives* 3.6, 29.4. R. M. Grant (*Zeitschrift für Religions- und Geistesgeschichte*, 4 [1952], 273) also defends this order by drawing attention to the "grammaticological" (?) use of *prohēgoumenos-kat' epakolouthēsin* in Stoic sources. But *prohēgoumenos* has nothing to do with the verb *proagein*. (b) Hope follows faith; love precedes hope (Lightfoot); the order faith, love, hope is found in 1 Thessalonians 1:3; Colossians 1:4-5. But this is very artificial linguistically. (c) Hope follows faith; love goes on ahead (for *proagein* of spartial precedence—both literal and figurative—see BAG, 708). In this case we are probably dealing with a reflection on 1 Corinthians 13:13 (faith, hope, love). There is no concern to relate these concepts in a particular way to one another; they form an inseparable triad; at most love (as in 1 Cor. 13) is "the greatest of these," to judge from the final remarks in the verse (cf. Ign. Eph. 9:1; 14:1; 2 Pet. 1:5-7). This interpretation is to be preferred. The two verbs—*epakolouthein* and *proagein*—are found together only here and in 1 Timothy 5:24 within the NT and Apostolic Fathers. In

IV. Table of duties I (4:1-3)

4 "The beginning *of all* difficulties is *the love of money.*"[1] *Knowing*, then, *that*[2] *"we brought nothing into the world* and, moreover, *can take nothing out,"*[3] let us arm with *"the arms of righteousness"*[4] and teach first ourselves to *walk in the commandment of the Lord;*[5] 2. then (teach) also *"your wives"*[6] (to walk) in the *faith, love, and purity*[7] *given*[8] them, *"showing affec-*

---

[1] 1 Tim. 6:10.   [2] See 1:3, n. 16.
[3] Tim. 6:7. Both von Campenhausen (*SHA*, 1951, 28) and Dibelius pp. 65–66 suggest that Polycarp quotes neither 1 Tim. 6:10 nor 1 Tim. 6:7. The former believes that Polycarp wrote the Pastorals and that these are repetitions of familiar thoughts. The latter suggests that the themes are so widespread in the diatribe that no interdependence is necessary. We may agree with Dibelius that the content is common coin; but the form especially of the second parallel is too closely related to be accounted for in this way. Moreover, we would be forced to assume that Polycarp and 1 Timothy were both in touch with a tradition that joined the two themes. As analysis of von Campenhausen's thesis goes beyond the limits of this commentary (see p. 5). It is to be noted, however, that the form of the second parallel shows improvement in detail in Polycarp's version of it. Such improvement may point (as in the Synoptic Gospels) to later refinement by a different hand. In 1 Tim. 6:7 an anomalous *hoti* (S*AG) joins the two clauses (cf. BAG, 593). Even if that is possibly a later dittography, Polycarp's *all' oude* ("not only this, but also") represents a refinement. (The significance of the formula "knowing that" is, in light of 6:1, ambiguous; but there seems to be a greater likelihood that our author follows it by material not of his own making).
[4] 2 Cor. 6:7 (Rom. 6:13).   [5] Luke 1:6.
[6] 1 Clem. 1:3.   [7] 1 Tim. 2:15; 4:12.   [8] Jude 3.

---

1 Timothy 5:24 a figurative application of their spacial meaning occurs (cf. *The Epitaph of Abercius*, 12).

4:1-3. A warning against love of money and encouragement to "arm with the arms of righteousness" is addressed to the male adults of the community (4:1). There follows the first section of a table of duties concerned with (1) wives, (2) children, (3) widows (4:2-3).

The significant warning against love of money prepares the way for the later discussion of Valens (11:1). Its appearance at this point has led commentators to assume that the question concerning righteousness (3:1-3) had to do only with moral problems. But we have seen that heresy is also involved. How, then, is the warning against love of money related to that against false teaching? Meinhold has suggested (PWK, XXI, 1686-1687) that Valens misused his office in the eyes of Polycarp and the Philippians by accepting a donation from Marcion of the same kind which the latter bestowed on the Roman church. Not only is Marcionite influence questionable (see on 7:1-2), but the theory also reads too much into the letter.

tion for their own husbands" ⁸ in complete fidelity and *"loving all men equally"* ⁹ in complete chastity, and to *"bring up their children with the discipline that issues in the fear of God";* ¹⁰ 3. (and

⁹ 1 Clem. 21:7 (Polycarp's form more compact).
¹⁰ 1 Clem. 21:6 (cf. 21:8; Sir. 1:27).

It seems likely to me that the two issues were more or less separate in the letter from the Philippians. Valens, however, was probably an embarrassment to the orthodox cause (Bauer, *Rechtgläubigkeit*, 77), and this may have prompted Polycarp to link the two issues. His point is this: Heresy and love of money are closely related (cf. 11:2). This is also the theory of the Pastorals (1 Tim. 6:3-5, 10, 11; Tit. 1:11); but the fact that Polycarp does not dare to link them as intimately as do the Pastorals indicates that Valens himself has no connection with heresy (see on 6:2-3; 11:2). Polycarp is saying in effect: You are having problems with false teaching because of moral weakness. Valens is to Polycarp only a signal example of this weakness; hence his warning to *all* the orders of the congregation against love of money (vs. 3; 5:2; 6:1). (It is not clear how Polycarp may have related this warning to the obvious fact that Valens' action was heartily disapproved; but he may well have been driven by the logic of his position to assume that the case of Valens pointed to hidden impulses in the congregation as a whole.) Here, as in 1 Timothy 6:10-11, righteousness is the antidote to the love of money which has brought men to wander from the faith. Polycarp proceeds to elaborate such righteousness in terms of a table of duties (4:1-6:3).

Polycarp's table of duties is related in scope to those of the Pastorals. The tables in Colossians 3:18-4:1; Ephesians 5:22-6:9; 1 Peter 2:18-3:7; Didache 4:9-11; and 1 Clement 1:3; 21:6-8 are briefer and are nearer to Stoic models in dealing only with the natural (as opposed to the ecclesiastical) orders. Polycarp's lists represent a reworking of many traditional (and possibly a few new) elements. There is no need to regard vs. 2 as directed against Marcion's asceticism (Meinhold, PWK, XXI, 1687). Nor is it likely that it prepares the way for the criticism of Valens' wife (Zahn, *Ignatius*, 297-298) since there is no mention of the love of money.

4:1. For the many parallels to 1 Timothy 6:10, 7 see Dibelius pp. 65-66. The closest are derived from the Stoic-Cynic ideal of self-sufficiency (cf. D.L. 6.50, 7.111; Seneca, *Ep.* 102.24-25; Philo, *De Specialibus Legibus* 1.294-295). *Ourselves:* Not presbyters; they are addressed for the first time in 6:1. Polycarp has in mind adult male members of the congregation. 4:2. *Your wives:* The change from the first to the second person does not necessarily indicate that Polycarp was celibate (Zahn, *Ignatius*, 337-338). The lack of grammatical symmetry is a reflection of the epistolary situation. *Given them:* The phrase probably modifies "love" and "purity" as well as "faith" in view

teach) *the widows* [11] *to be sober* [12] about *the faith of the Lord,* [13] *praying constantly* [14] *for all men,* [15] *being far* [16] from all *slander,* [17] *evil speech,* [18] *false witness,* [19] *love of money,* [20] *and evil of any kind,* [21] *knowing that* [22] they are an altar of God and that all

[11] 1 Tim. 5:3-6.
[12] 1 Clem. 1:3.
[13] Jas. 2:1.
[14] 1 Thess. 5:17; Ign. Eph. 10:1.
[15] 1 Tim. 2:2; 1 Clem. 56:1.
[16] See 3:3, n. 19.
[17] 1 Tim. 3:11; Tit. 2:3.
[18] See 2:2, n. 23.
[19] See 2:2, n. 24.
[20] See 2:2, n. 22.
[21] Job 2:3; 1 Clem. 17:3 (cf. 1 Thess. 5:22).
[22] Jas. 1:3 (*gignōskontes hoti*); Rom. 6:6.

of the single article (B-D, 144; for the position of the modifier see Ign. Eph. 1:2; Mag. 14:1). *Loving:* For *agapan* of a less intimate affection see Xenophon, *Mem.* 2.7.9, 12. 4:3. *Widows:* No doubt real widows (unlike the "virgins called widows" of Ign. Smyrn. 13:1) who gain support from the community and in turn spend their lives in prayer (1 Tim. 5:3-11; cf. Ed. Schweizer, *Church Order* [Naperville, 1961], 86). They form an order within the church and are to be distinguished from widows who are simply members of the congregation in need of help (6:1; Ign. Smyrn. 6:2; Polyc. 4:1). *To be sober about:* Polycarp's use of *sōphronein peri* probably transposes into the moral realm the significance of the expression for the intellect in, say, Xenophon, *Mem.* 1.1.20: Socrates is said not "*to hold sound opinions concerning the gods.*" If this interpretation is correct, there is no hint here of a teaching function (Lightfoot). In 1 Clement 1:3 (and elsewhere) the word has special reference to chastity (cf. 1 Tim. 5:11-15). The widows' behavior is to bring no discredit on the faith. *An altar of God:* A figurative use of the term attested to here for the first time. Elsewhere altar is used of the pure heart and mind (Sextus 46b [Pythagorean parallels in H. Chadwick, *The Sentences of Sextus* (Cambridge, Eng., 1959), 166], Philo, *De Specialibus Legibus* 1.287 [note that a nearby passage, 1.294-295, offers one of the best parallels to vs. 1—that is, 1 Tim. 6:7]; Clement, *Str.* 6.60.2; 7.14 ff.; 7.32.5). Polycarp demands such purity of widows but also of others. Widows in particular may be connected with the altar because of their concern with prayer (cf. Rev. 5:8; 8:3, 4; 11:1); note the Rabbinic teaching that prayer is of a value equal to that of the cultus (*Sifre on Deuteronomy* 41, f.80a [G. F. Moore, *Judaism* (Cambridge, Mass., 1927), II, 218]: "Just as the worship of the *altar* is called worship, so *prayer* is called worship"). For later developments of the theme see Tertullian, *Ad Uxorem* 1.7; ApCo 2.26; 4.3; Pseudo-Ignatius, *Tarsians* 9:1; Methodius, *Symposium* 5.6-8. *Offerings are carefully inspected:* An effort to translate the single word *mōmoskopeitai*, which recalls the OT sacrificial system (see 1 Clem. 41:2, which also refers to the altar). For a figurative application of the noun see Philo, *De Agricultura* 130; Clement, *Str.* 4.117.4.

offerings are carefully inspected,²³ and *"nothing escapes him either of their reflections or thoughts"* ²⁴ and of *"the hidden things of the heart."* ²⁵

V. Table of duties II (5:1-6:3)

5 *Knowing, then, that*¹ *"God is not mocked."*² *we ought*³ *to walk*⁴ *worthily*⁵ *of his commandment*⁶ and glory. 2. *Likewise* (must) *deacons*⁷ (be) *blameless*⁸ *before his*⁹ righteousness as *ministers of God*¹⁰ *and Christ*¹¹ and *not of men:*¹² not *slanderers*,¹³ not *insincere*,¹⁴ not *lovers of money*,¹⁵ *temperate*¹⁶ in everything, *compassionate*,¹⁷ attentive, *walking* according to *the truth*¹⁸ of the Lord, who was *minister of all;*¹⁹ and should we

²³ 1 Clem. 41:2.	²⁴ 1 Clem. 21:3.	²⁵ 1 Cor. 14:25.
¹ See 1:3, n. 16.	² Gal. 6:7.	³ 1 John 4:11.
⁴ 1 John 2:6.	⁵ 1 Thess. 2:12.	⁶ 2 John 6.
⁷ 1 Tim. 3:8.		
⁸ 1 Thess. 3:13; Phil. 2:15; Eph. 1:4; Luke 1:6.		
⁹ Eph. 1:4.		¹⁰ 2 Cor. 6:4.
¹¹ 2 Cor. 11:23; Ign. Smyrn. 10:1.		¹² Gal. 1:1.
¹³ See 4:3, n. 17.		¹⁴ 1 Tim. 3:8.
¹⁵ See 2:2, n. 22.		¹⁶ Tit. 1:8.
¹⁷ 1 Pet. 3:8; Eph. 4:32.		¹⁸ 3 John 4.

¹⁹ Mark 9:35; but closer in content to Mark 10:45; Matt. 20:28; "the application is so natural as to make it impossible to treat the passage as serious evidence for Polycarp's use of Mark" (*The New Testament in the Apostolic Fathers* [Oxford, 1905], 101).

5:1-6:3. A brief exhortation (5:1) suggests a break at this point. Note also the different grammatical pattern in the second part of the table of duties (5:2-6:1). This part has to do with (1) deacons, (2) young men, (3) virgins, (4) elders. The exhortation to elders is elaborated to include a brief discussion of (*a*) forgiveness and (*b*) false teachers (6:2-3). For the significance of Polycarp's failure to mention a bishop see p. 7.

In the elaboration concerning forgiveness and false teachers Polycarp brings together once again the two main practical issues of the letter. His purpose in doing so seems to be to make his position on both clear. The exhortation to forgive is closely related to the problem of the love of money, and hence reminds us again of Valens whose case would be decided no doubt primarily by presbyters. Polycarp is preparing the way for his later exhortation to clemency (11:4-12:1). The suggestion is not that Valens had anything to do directly with the false teachers who are also mentioned (6:3). It is precisely because Valens has nothing to do with heresy that he is not numbered with the

please him [20] *in the present world,*[21] we shall *gain* [22] also *the world to come,*[23] just as he promised us *to raise us from the dead,*[24] and that if we *"live worthily as his citizens,"* [25] *we shall also reign with him,*[26] if only we believe. 3. Likewise (must) also *the young men* [27] (be) *blameless* [28] in all things, caring above all for purity and *restraining* [29] themselves *from every evil;* [30] for *it is good* [31] to refrain from *worldly lusts,*[32] because *"every lust wars against* the spirit" [33] and *"neither will fornicators nor effeminates nor homosexuals* inherit the kingdom of God" [34] nor those who *do what is improper;* [35] therefore it is necessary to *abstain from all* [36] these things and to *be subject to the elders* [37] and *deacons as to God and Christ.*[38] *Virgins* [39] (ought) to walk *"in a spotless and holy conscience."* [40]

[20] Heb. 11:5-6; 1 Clem. 41:1.
[21] 1 Tim. 6:17; 2 Tim. 4:10; Tit. 2:13.
[22] Col. 3:24.
[23] 1 Tim. 4:8; Heb. 6:5; Eph. 1:21.
[24] 2 Cor. 4:14; Rom. 8:11.   [25] 1 Clem. 21:1.
[26] 2 Tim. 2:12. Part of a "faithful saying" which may have been known to Polycarp. He possibly understood it as a word of Christ; but the verb, "he promised," cannot be pressed (cf. Justin, *Apol.* 1.10.2).
[27] 1 Pet. 5:5.   [28] See 5:2, n. 8.   [29] Jas. 1:26.
[30] See 4:3, n. 21.   [31] 1 Cor. 7:1.
[32] Tit. 2:12 (cf. 1 John 2:16).
[33] 1 Pet. 2:11 (cf. Gal. 5:17).   [34] 1 Cor. 6:9-10.
[35] Job 27:6; 34:12; Prov. 30:20; 2 Macc. 14:23; Luke 23:41.
[36] 1 Thess. 5:22.
[37] 1 Pet. 5:5 (cf. 1 Clem. 1:3; 57:1).
[38] Ign. Magn. 2; 6:1; 13:2; Trall. 2:2; 3:1; Smyrn. 8:1; Polyc. 6:1.
[39] Ign. Smyrn. 13:1.   [40] 1 Clem. 1:3.

---

heathen (cf. 11:2-3) and can be forgiven and recalled. The false teachers, on the other hand, are to be entirely avoided.

The apparent emphasis (6:3) on the prophetic proclamation concerning the coming of Christ and its unity with the apostolic gospel (cf. Eph. 2:20) has been taken by Meinhold (PWK, XXI, 1685) to point to a rejection of the view of the OT and the God of the OT propounded by Marcion. Similar views, however, are found elsewhere (Simon Magus in Irenaeus, *Adv. haer.* 1.23.3; Hippolutus, *Ref.* 6.19.7; ApCo 6.10.1; cf. G. Thomas 90.12-18), and even a more ambiguous position like that of Basilides (Irenaeus, *Adv. haer.* 2.35.2) and the Valentinians (4.35.1) would suffice to explain such an emphasis. In any event, the parallels in n. 67 suggest that the theme may be more traditional than polemical.

5:2. *The present world:* An expression peculiar in primitive

6 And *the presbyters*[41] (must) also (be) *compassionate,*[42] *merciful*[43] to all men, *"bringing back those that have erred,"*[44] *looking after*[45] all *the sick,*[46] not neglecting *the widow*[47] or orphan or poor man;[48] but *"providing always for what is good before God and men,"*[49] abstaining from all [36] anger,[50] favoritism,[51] *unjust judgment;*[52] *being far*[53] from all *love of money,*[54] not quick to believe evil of anyone,[55] not *severe in judgment,*[56]

[41] 1 Tim. 5:17.   [42] See 5:2, n. 17.
[43] Matt. 5:7.   [44] Ezek. 34:4, 16 (cf. 1 Pet. 2:25; 1 Clem. 59:4).
[45] Ezek. 34:11.   [46] Matt. 25:36, 43.
[47] Ign. Polyc. 4:1.
[48] Acts 6:1; 9:39, 41; Jas. 1:27; Barn. 20:2; Hermas, Vis. 2.4.3; Mand. 8:10; Sim. 1.8; 5.3.7; Ign. Smyrn. 6:2.
[49] Prov. 3:4 (cf. 2 Cor. 8:21; Rom. 12:17; the quotation is most closely related to the text of the OT itself; the NT passages may well have stimulated interest in it at some point in Polycarp's reflections).
[36] 1 Thess. 5:22.   [50] Eph. 4:31; Col. 3:8.   [51] Jas. 2:1.
[52] Lev. 19:15; Job 6:29 (A).
[53] See 3:3, n. 19.   [54] See 2:2, n. 22.
[55] Cf. 1 Tim. 5:19.   [56] Sir. 6:5.

Christian literature to Polycarp and the Pastorals (see n. 23). Three other words are also found only here and in the Pastorals within the NT and the Apostolic Fathers: *egkratēs, diabolos* (as an adjective), *dilogos* (Campenhausen, *SHA*, 1951, 25-26). *If only we believe:* Reigning with God is contingent in some way both on living worthily and believing. The same themes (among others) occur in Justin, *Apol.* 1.10.1-2. There what we have been "taught," what we are "convinced of," and what we "believe" is this: that only those who live virtuously will be received by God and reign with him. Despite the difference in context, it is not unlikely that the same connection of ideas is presupposed here. **5:3.** *Restraining:* Literally "bridling" (Jas. 1:26; 3:2; Hermas, *Mand.* 12.1.1; cf. Philo, *Quod Deterius* 23). *Elders and deacons:* These two offices obviously stand somewhat apart despite the fact that they are interwoven in the table of duties with the "natural" orders; at the same time we are not far from the ambivalent way in which the term "elders" may be used both of officials and of old men in contrast with young men (1 Pet. 5:1, 5; 1 Clem. 1:3). **6:1.** *Widow or orphan:* A widespread concern both in Judaism (e.g., Exodus Rabba 30.8) and early Christianity (see nn. 47-48 and Justin, *Apol.* 1.67.6). Widows, orphans, and the afflicted are mentioned together in Ignatius, Smyrnaeans 6:2 and Hermas, Similitudes 5.3.7. *Not quick to believe evil of anyone:* It may be significant that the parallel in 1 Timothy 5:19 specifies "presbyter" in this connection. This increases the likelihood that Polycarp is here anticipating the

knowing that[57] "we are all *debtors* of *sin*."[58] 2. If, then, we entreat the Lord *"to forgive us, we* ought *also to forgive";*[59] for we are *before the eyes of the Lord*[60] and of God, and *"we* must *all stand at the judgment seat* of Christ"[61] and "each must *give*

---

[57] See 1:3, n. 16.

[58] The introductory formula suggests that we are dealing at least with a piece of proverbial wisdom; and, as we have seen, it is possible that Polycarp uses it to introduce apostolic material. In fact, the language here rises above the useful flatness of Polycarp's style. Some think the passage may be derived from a lost source. Others that it represents a kind of inversion of the thought in Rom. 8:12. R. M. Grant has suggested that it refers onward to the beginning of 6:2 ("if, then, . . .") and thus serves to introduce tradition of the Synoptic type. He thinks that there is a possible parallel to this in 4:3, where a similar formula may refer onward to the quotation derived from 1 Clem. 21:3. I have been convinced, however, by the Rev. L. C. Crockett that Polycarp has in mind Matt. 6:12 ("And forgive us our debts, As we also have forgiven our *debtors*")—probably with echoes of Luke 11:4 ("and forgive us our *sins*, for we ourselves also forgive every *debtor* of ours"). From this Polycarp has deduced (otherwise why pray thus?) that we are all "debtors of sin"—that is, men in need of forgiveness. What immediately follows in 6:2 supports this conclusion. It presupposes the same Matthean context (see n. 59) and may well be closely connected with what precedes by the "if then" (cf. Matt. 6:23; Luke 11:36; 12:26).

[59] Matt. 6:12, 14-15.

[60] Isa. 1:16 (1 Clem. 8:4).

[61] Rom. 14:10. Various authorities (Sc L P Syr-vg, h Marcion Tertullian) read "the judgment seat of Christ" (probably a contamination from 2 Cor. 5:10).

---

discussion of the presbyter Valens. *Debtors of sin:* Polycarp's main purpose is to encourage a willingness on the part of the elders to forgive by increasing the awareness of their own (continued) need of divine forgiveness. The function of the theme of judgment in 6:2 seems to be to effect such awareness. (Only in a subordinate sense could it be taken to imply opposition to heretical views such as those referred to in 7:1.) To an extent it is fair to say that "man is still regarded as on the debit side of an account with God" (Torrance p. 95). At the same time, however, there is presupposed a confidence that our debt of sin is in fact forgiven if we ourselves forgive. Although the argument displays a greater reliance on the created potentialities of man than is the case with Paul, it is not far from the Synoptic teaching which it echoes. It is assumed that the realization of such potentialities is impossible without the work of Christ (cf. 8:1). 6:2–3. *We entreat the Lord . . . him . . . he:* It is best to understand a reference to God in all three cases (despite the intervening contrast between "the Lord" and "God"). Then the allusion to Psalm 2:11 may be regarded as "his" commandment (Bauer p. 290).

account of himself."[62] 3. So then, let us *serve him with fear*[63] and all *reverence*[64] *as he* himself *commanded*,[65] and the *apostles who preached the gospel*[66] to us and *the prophets who proclaimed beforehand the coming*[67] of our Lord; (let us be) *fervent for what is good*,[68] *abstaining from*[69] temptations and *false brethren*[70] *and those bearing hypocritically the name of the Lord*,[71] *who mislead*[72] *vain men.*[73]

VI. Docetism (7:1-2)

7 For "everyone who *does not confess that Jesus Christ came in*

[62] Rom. 14:12. [63] Ps. 2:11 (cf. 2:1, n. 2).
[64] Heb. 12:28. [65] Jer. 13:5.
[66] Acts 14:14-15; 1 Pet. 1:12.
[67] Acts 7:52; 1 Clem. 17:1.
[68] 1 Pet. 3:13; Tit. 2:14.
[69] See 2.2, n. 19.
[70] 2 Cor. 11:26; Gal. 2:4.
[71] 1 Tim. 4:2; Ign. Eph. 7:1.
[72] 1 Tim. 6:10. [73] Jas. 2:20.

7:1-2. This chapter falls into two parts: (1) a rejection of the Docetic views of the "false brethren" and (2) an exhortation to return to traditional teaching.

The following notes are intended primarily to demonstrate the unlikelihood that Polycarp is opposing Marcion in this letter. Many commentators emphasize the fact that no reference is made to Marcion's most characteristic teaching: the rejection of the OT and the God of the OT. Harrison pp. 183-206 constructed an elaborate theory by which he sought to prove that this doctrine was derived by Marcion from Cerdo at a later date. Meinhold (PWK, XXI, 1685) thinks this theory unnecessary since he regards the reference to the prophets in 6:2 as polemically oriented. We have seen how uncertain that is; in any event, it would represent a remarkably anemic attack in the case of Marcion.

The polemic here is not unlike the anti-Docetic passages in the letters of John and Ignatius. It is the discussion of righteousness in 3:1-3 that introduces a new note. But it is by no means clear evidence of Marcionite heresy.

7:1. The fleshly nature of Christ was early denied in Gnostic circles (Irenaeus, *Adv. haer.* 1.24.2; cf. Ign. Trall. 9:1-2). For Marcion's Docetism see Harnack p. 124. *The testimony* (witness) *of the cross:* The tenuous parallel, 1 John 5:6-9, suggests that this is the witness of God through the cross to his Son. More simply, it may refer to the witness that the cross is felt to give to the reality of Christ's suffering. The statement is directed against Docetists who believed that

the flesh is antichrist;"[1] and anyone who does not confess[2] the testimony of the cross "is of the devil";[3] and anyone who perverts the sayings of the Lord to suit his own lusts[4] and says that there

---

[1] 1 John 4:2-3; 2 John 7. Von Campenhausen regards these themes as derived from a common anti-Gnostic ecclesiastical tradition (SHA, 1951, 40-41). But the use here of 1-2 John is regarded as undeniable by W. von Loewenich, Das Johannes-Verständnis im zweiten Jahrhundert (Giessen, 1932), 23.
[2] 1 John 4:3.   [3] 1 John 3:8 (cf. John 8:44).
[4] 2 Tim. 4:3; cf. 2 Pet. 3:3.

Christ did not really suffer (Ign. Trall. 10; Smyrn. 2). (This accords with the thesis of N. Brox, Zeuge und Märtyrer [Munich, 1961], 224, 234-235: the use of *martyrion* here links the common notion of "witness" as "witness to a fact" with the later technical sense "martyrdom"; for "the suffering and dying of the martyr is a witness for the true bodily nature of Christ and his truly experienced passion.") According to Harnack pp. 125-126, Marcion's denial of a fleshly body of Christ did not prevent him from stressing the reality of Christ's suffering; but it must be admitted that Marcion's opponents missed this nuance (Tertullian, De Carne Christi 5; Hippolytus, Ref. 10.19.3-4). *Perverts the sayings of the Lord:* Meinhold (PWK, XXI, 1686) draws attention to Marcion's criticism of the evangelic tradition. *Logia tou Kyriou* probably does refer to sayings ("oracles") of Jesus (Lampe p. 806; Polycarp usually has Christ in mind when he says "Lord"; and see Clement, Quis Dives 3.1; in Irenaeus, Adv. haer. 1. Praef. 1 the expression is ambiguous especially in light of the "Dominical oracles" of 1.8.1). Polycarp's quotations in verse 2 strengthen the impression that he is particularly concerned about the evangelical tradition at this point. But Marcion's NT criticism also applied to Paul; consequently it is equally possible that Polycarp singles out one element from an even wider range of exegetical perversions. (Note the separate treatment that Irenaeus even in his day proposed to give to "the words of the Lord" [Adv. haer. 4. Praef. 1; 4.41.4].) The verb *methodeuein,* moreover, probably refers simply to the "twisting" of language (Lampe p. 839) rather than to the removal of texts. It is clear that the use of the flexible term "oracles" for Scripture (Heb. 5:12; 1 Clem. 53:1) and the words of Jesus was one of the bridges over which the canonization of the NT proceeded; for even when used of the OT it retained an emphasis on the divine utterances themselves rather than on the collection of sacred writings (with which they were thought to coincide) and thus made possible the recognition of a new covenant of equal authority with the old, especially since the divinity of the Lord's utterances was taken for granted. In verse 2, however, the formula of citation ("as the Lord said"; see also 2:3, nn. 26, 29) does not suggest (though in light of Irenaeus' usage, for example, does not preclude)

is neither a resurrection nor a judgment—that man is the first-born of Satan! 2. Therefore let us *give up the vanity*[5] of the crowd and false teachings and *return*[6] to the word *handed on to us from the beginning*,[7] "*being sober unto prayer*"[8] and per-

[5] See 2:1, n. 3.
[6] 1 Clem. 19:2; Jude 3.
[ʜ] 1 Clem. 9:1 (see n. 5).
[8] 1 Pet. 4:7.

---

canonical status for the Gospels. (The attempt to find a reference here to OT "oracles" concerning Jesus is—in light of the parallels above—forced.) *Lusts:* The usual meaning of *epithymia* (cf. BAG, 293, and the use of the term in 5:3). Polycarp seems to be suggesting that these heretical views are intended as grounds for loose living. Although there is probably misrepresentation and exaggeration here, it would have been difficult to use such language of the ascetic Marcion. Harrison pp. 177-178, to be sure, insists that the term refers to perverse belief as in 2 Timothy 4:3 ("to suit their own likings," RSV). But Polycarp's use of *pros* instead of *kata* puts some distance between the two passages; and in 2 Peter 3.3 we find even the expression *kata tas idias epithymias* used in the sense "according to their passions" with immediate reference to men who scoff at the prediction of Christ's coming. *Resurrection:* Commonly denied (or reinterpreted) by the Gnostics (cf. 2 Tim. 2:18; 2 Clem. 9:1; Justin, *Apol.* 1.26.4; *Dial.* 80; Irenaeus, *Adv. haer.* 1.23.5, 2.31.2; Tertullian, *De Resurrectione Carnis* 19; cf. Zahn, *Introduction,* II, 129); so also Marcion (Harnack pp. 136-141). *Judgment:* Such a denial was traced by the church to the followers of Simon Magus (ApCo 6.10.1; cf. Irenaeus, *Adv. haer.* 1.23.3; Hippolytus, *Ref.* 6.19.7). The teaching springs from the inner logic of Gnosticism as a whole (cf. Irenaeus, *Adv haer.* 1.13.6; 2.19.2; 2.22.1-2; Origen, *Commentary on John* 20.358-62). Interestingly enough, however, Marcion never denied that there would be a day of judgment, and he even allowed for a sort of judging activity of God "*nolendo et . . . prohibendo*" (Tertullian, *Adversus Marcionem* 1.27); he also retained Romans 2:16, quoted by Polycarp above (Harnack pp. 137-139). Naturally such nuances may have been lost on his opponents (cf. Irenaeus, *Adv. haer.* 3.25.2-3); nevertheless, denial of "the judgment" is not the sort of charge that is heard against Marcion. *First-born of Satan!:* According to Irenaeus (*Adv. haer.* 3.3.4; Eusebius, *H.E.* 4.14.7), this term was applied by Polycarp to Marcion when they met. This took place presumably not too long before Marcion's arrival in Rome *ca.* A.D. 140 (Harnack pp. 24-26). It has been argued that this proves either that our letter is not authentic, or that it comes from a later period than is usually assumed, or that chapters 1-12 come from a later period than chapters 13-14 (Harrison). Such conclusions are not necessary. The charges in this chapter are not directed against specifically Marcionite doctrine; and it is quite possible that Polycarp would have made a remark like this more than once

severing[9] *in fasts*,[10] in our entreaties beseeching *the all-seeing God*[11] "*to lead us not into temptation,*"[12] as the Lord said: "*The spirit is willing, but the flesh is weak.*"[13]

VII. The imitation of Christ (8:1-2)

8 Let us *persevere*,[1] then, *constantly*[2] in *our hope*[3] and the

---

[9] Rom. 12:12. [10] 2 Cor. 11:27.
[11] 1 Clem. 55:6; 64:1. [12] Matt. 6:13 (cf. Luke 11:4).
[13] The connection of the petition from the Lord's Prayer with the saying about the spirit and the flesh in vs. 2 is anticipated already in the Gospels (Mark. 14:38; Matt. 26:41). Since this connection appears secondary, it is reasonable to suppose that Polycarp derived it from the written Gospels (Koester pp. 114–115).

[1] Col. 4:2. [2] 1 Thess. 5:17.
[3] Col. 1:27; 1 Tim. 1:1; Ign. Magn. 11; Trall. inscr.; 2:2; cf. Ascension of Isaiah 4:13.

(Harnack p. 5*, n. 4; Bauer pp. 291-292) especially since he was given to repetition (Eusebius, *H.E.* 5.20.7). Note also that the expression was later applied to Simon Magus (Ps.-Ign. Trall. 11). The request "Recognize us!"–to which Polycarp answers, "I recognize, I recognize the first-born of Satan"–may have been artificially constructed to provide a framework for the bon mot derived from his letter (Simonetti, *GIF*, 9 [1956], 344). To this it may be replied (Harnack p. 5*, n. 3) that Polycarp's answer to the proconsul in the Martyrdom of Polycarp 9:2 has the same "biting irony" and that this vouches for the authenticity of the apophthegm. It is doubtful, however, that the two accounts can be compared so directly. Twisting the obvious meaning of the judge's question occurs elsewhere in the acts of the martyrs (e.g., Mart. Carp. 28-32; Mart. Pion. 5.3-4), and in Philostratus, *Vit. Apollon.* 8.4 we even find a use of gesture analogous to that in Mart. Polyc. 9:2. Our views are confirmed by N. A. Dahl (in *Apophoreta* [Berlin, 1964], 70-84). He traces the phrase "firstborn of Satan" to Jewish sources, argues that it originally referred to Cain (cf. Gen. 4:1), and suggests that in Polycarp we have a reapplication of it which may well have belonged to standard anti-Gnostic polemic. (He also thinks it lies behind John 8:44.) 7:2. *The vanity of the crowd:* See notes on 2:1. *Fasts . . . temptation . . . flesh:* See n. 13. Fasting is not mentioned in Matthew 26:41, but it was early associated with prayer (Luke 2:37; Acts 13:3; 14:23; cf. 1 Thess. 5:6; 1 Pet. 5:8). Although the rejecting of specific Gnostic doctrines has been left behind, it is improbable that Polycarp would ask for fasting as a deterrent to heresy if he had been speaking of Marcion; for the latter made much of the same practice (Harnack pp. 149-150).

8:1–2. Corollaries of the avoidance of Docetic teaching are elabo-

pledge[4] of our righteousness, *which is Christ Jesus*,[3] who "*bore our sins in his own body on the cross,*"[5] "*who did no sin, nor was any deceit found in his mouth*";[6] but he *endured*[7] *all things for us*[8] *that we might live*[9] *in him.*[10] 2. *Let us be imitators,*[11] then, of *his endurance,*[12] and if we *suffer for his name, let us glorify him.*[13] For this is the "*example*"[14] which he set in himself; and *this we learned to believe.*[15]

[4] Eph. 1:14; 2 Cor. 1:22; 5:5.
[6] 1 Pet. 2:22 (cf. Isa. 53:9).
[8] Ign. Polyc. 3:2.
[9] 1 Pet. 2:24 (cf. 1 John 4:9).
[11] 1 Thess. 1:6; 1 Cor. 11:1 (cf. Ign. Eph. 10:3).
[12] 2 Thess. 3:5.
[13] 1 Pet. 3:14; 4:15-16; Acts 9:16; Hermas, Sim. 9.28.2-6.
[14] 1 Pet. 2:21 (the context suggests that the term is drawn directly from this passage; but see also 1 Clem. 5:7; 16:17; 33:8).
[15] 1 Cor. 15:11 (*houtōs episteusate*).

[5] 1 Pet. 2:24.
[7] See 1:2, n. 11.
[10] Rom. 6:11.

---

rated in this and the following two chapters. Here two points are made: (1) We must hold fast to the righteousness gained for us by Christ through his supreme endurance (vs. 1) and (2) we must become imitators of this endurance (vs. 2). Both are variations on a single theme.

The whole chapter underscores the reality of the suffering of Christ. This is done by carrying forward the interpretation of righteousness which provides (as it did in 3:1-6:3) the answer to heretical vanity (7:2; cf. 2:1). Christ's endurance and man's perseverance are closely interrelated. This adds weight to the suggestion that Polycarp understood the Docetism of the errorists as leading to undisciplined living. The preservation of righteousness, in his mind, may even involve a suffering like that of the Lord. To this he turns more directly in the next chapter.

Von Campenhausen *Idee* p. 79 regards this passage along with 1:1 and 10:1 as one of the earliest formulations of the catholic idea of martyrdom. He sees it as a departure from the NT, though he recognizes affinities with 1 Peter 2:21. The basic difficulty is that "the historically oriented idea of following after Christ (*Nachfolge*) is suppressed . . . by the thought of imitation (*Nachahmung*)." The death of the martyr, not his witness, is put into the foreground. Obedience is turned into a heroic virtue. (See further Mart. Polyc. 1:1-2)

8:1 *Which is Christ Jesus:* The reference is to "hope and the pledge" not to "righteousness" in view of the fact that "our hope" is Christ in the parallels (see n. 3). *Pledge:* Or "first instalment," "down payment" (BAG, 109). "Christ is thought of as the pledge of a righteousness which *we* must persevere to fulfil" (Torrance pp. 92-93).

VIII. The martyrs (9:1-2)

9 *I exhort all of you, then,*[1] *to obey*[2] *the word of righteousness*[3] *and to exercise*[4] *all endurance,*[5] *which you also saw*[6] *before your eyes*[7] not only in the blessed Ignatius and Zosimus and Rufus, but also in others from among you and *in*[6] Paul himself and *the rest of the apostles;*[8] 2. *being persuaded that*[9] *all these*[10] *"did not run in vain,"*[11] but *in faith and righteousness,*[12] and that they are

[1] Rom. 12:1, etc.	[2] Tit. 3:1.	[3] Heb. 5:13.
[4] Acts 24:16.	[5] Col. 1:11.	[6] Phil. 4:9.
[7] Gal. 3:1.	[8] Acts 2:37.	[9] 2 Tim. 1:12.
[10] Heb. 11:39.		[11] Phil. 2:16 (cf. Gal. 2:2).
[12] 1 Clem. 42:5 (Isa. 60:17); but see n. 13.		

The death of Christ has to do fundamentally with past sins; Christians are expected henceforth to obey God (to endure) and thus to perserve the status won for them by Christ. In the NT the pledge is connected with the Spirit of God (see n. 4); in Polycarp, with Jesus Christ and the work of forgiveness; hence man is thrown back on his own responsibility and resources after his sins have been forgiven.

9:1-2. The Philippians are exhorted to emulate the righteousness and endurance which was exemplified in the martyrs from Paul to Ignatius (vs. 1) in the assurance that such "faith" and "righteousness" met with divine approval (vs. 2).

The problem of the integrity of the letter (see below) should not cause the reader to lose sight of the main purpose of the passage. It carries forward the thought of 8:2. Faith and righteousness are to be understood in terms of "endurance"—even to the point of martyrdom if necessary.

Polycarp clearly feels that the whole line of early Christian martyrs lends support to his interpretation of the faith. They make an antinomian interpretation of "righteousness" impossible. Hence the concluding remark that they did not love the present world (vs. 2). At the same time there is no suggestion that they hated the body; indeed, an anti-Docetic note may be reflected (*a*) in the concluding reference to the resurrected Lord and (*b*) in the remark that they did not run in vain; for the latter probably should be understood against the background of Ignatius' complaint that martyrdom would make no sense if Christ did not truly suffer (Ign. Trall. 10).

9:1. *Zosimus and Rufus:* The names are both found in *CIG* (Boeckh), 192, 244, 1969, 3664; the name Valens also in 1969; all three names in *CIL*, III, 633 (from Philippi); Rufus in Romans 16:13; Mark 15:21. They plainly were not Philippians in light of the antithesis. At the same time Ignatius never mentions them. They may have been added to the party after the writing of his letters. Zahn notes that (at about the same time?) Pliny was sending Bithynian

"in their due place"[13] *beside the Lord*[14] *with whom they also suffered.*[15] *For they did not "love the present world"*[16] *but him who died for us and was raised by God because of us.*[17]

[13] 1 Clem. 5:4 (cf. 1 Clem. 5:6, "faith," and 5:7, "righteousness," "endurance," "example").
[14] Ps. 130:7; Prov. 15:11.
[15] Rom. 8:17; Ign. Smyrn. 4:2.
[16] 2 Tim. 4:20 (cf. Polyc. Phil. 5:2).   [17] Ign. Rom. 6:1.

Christians to Rome (*Ep.* 10.96.4). *Others:* Polycarp's vagueness may indicate that he knows only what he has deduced from Philippians 1:28-30. *Apostles:* Probably the "twelve," in contrast to a wider group including Paul. 9:2. *All these:* This is the key passage in Harrison's theory that we have before us two letters to the Philippians: chapters 1-12 and 13-14. In this chapter Ignatius and his companions are clearly among the dead (Harrison pp. 148-154; the parallel to 1 Clem. 5:4 may be taken to strengthen this interpretation); in 13:2 Polycarp does not seem to know whether they are alive or dead. We shall see later that the interpretation of 13:2 is itself uncertain. Here I should like to point out that it is not right to press Polycarp's words in this chapter for three reasons: (*a*) The Philippians saw Ignatius and his companions "before (their) eyes"— which presupposes a fresh memory of the martyrs; but there would hardly be any who had actually seen Paul (compare the careful expression used of Paul in 3:2) and "the rest of the apostles." Clearly Polycarp's attention shifts as the sentence proceeds. (*b*) The construction "not only . . . but also" almost always puts much greater emphasis on the second member of the sentence (cf. Matt. 21:21; John 5:18; Acts 19:27; 26:29; 27:10; Rom. 1:32); and when it is followed by another clause, as here, the latter usually has reference primarily, if not exclusively, to the second member (cf. 4 Macc. 2:4-5; John 17:20; Rom. 4:16-17; Phil. 2:27). (*c*) The allusion to 1 Clement 5:4 ("in their due place"), which is about Paul and Peter (leader of the "rest of the apostles"; cf. B. Altaner, *Historisches Jahrbuch*, 69 [1949], 28), increases the likelihood that the reference to having gone to "their due place" applies only to those mentioned at the end of verse 1. Polycarp's desire to broaden his appeal to include the whole range of early Christian martyrs has caused him to push the adversative element in "not only . . . but also" further than usual. We are not denying that "all these" includes Ignatius and his companions; but we are suggesting that everything that follows need not be taken to have direct reference to them. Similarly, "you also saw before your eyes" certainly controls grammatically both the "not only" and the "but also"; there can be no doubt that in the case of Paul and the "rest of the apostles" we could apply much more naturally the words of 1 Clement 5:3—"Let us *set before our eyes* the good apostles." The concern for pastoral exhorta-

IX. The brotherhood (10:1-3)

10* *Stand firm,*[1] *then, in these things*[2] *and follow the example*[3] *of the Lord, strong in the faith and immoveable,*[4] *affectionate to the brotherhood,*[5] *devoted to one another,*[6] *united in the truth,*[7] *serving one another*[8] *with the gentleness of the Lord,*[9] *despising*

---

* At this point the Greek portion of the text ends, and the Latin begins.
[1] Eph. 6:14 (cf. Ign. Polyc. 3:1). [2] 1 Tim. 4:15.
[3] 1 Pet. 2:21. [4] Col. 1:23 (1 Cor. 15:58).
[5] 1 Pet. 3:8 or 2:17; the Vulgate's rendering of the former suggests that it is the more likely allusion.
[6] The Vulgate's rendering of Rom. 12:10 suggests that it is the more likely allusion (cf. John 13:34; 15:12, 17; Rom. 13:8). It is unlikely that the two phrases (nn. 5, 6) should be run together: "devoted to one another with brotherly affection," and thus show dependence on Rom. 12:10 throughout.
[7] 3 John 8.
[8] The possible reference to Rom. 12:10 above (see n. 6) has suggested to many that these words (*alterutri praestolantes*) are connected with another phrase in Rom. 12:10—*tē timē allēlous prohēgoumenoi*. *Praestolari* usually means "await." Its use here may represent an extension of its meaning in the direction of "anticipate"—hence, "outdoing one another." There is another possibility: According to Aelius Donatus (*Eunuchus* 5.5.5) the word means *praesto esse* or *apparere* ("be at hand," "appear," or "wait on")—that is (he further explains), *obsequi* ("submit to"). "Await," then, becomes "wait on." It is possible that the Latin translator was rendering a phrase echoing something like the *dia tēs agapēs douleuete allēlois* of Gal. 5:13 (hence, "serving one another").
[9] 2 Cor. 10:1. [10] Matt. 18:10. [11] Prov. 3:28.

---

tion, not the desire for a clearly articulated historical statement, gives shape to the passage. We may hope that this exegesis will buttress the usual defense of the integrity of the letter (see on 13:1-2).

10:1–3. The imitation of Christ in the case of those not compelled to face martyrdom is articulated in terms of (*a*) loving the brotherhood (vss. 1-2) and (thereby?) (*b*) giving to the Gentiles no cause to blaspheme God (vss. 2-3).

The *ergo* of verse 1 plays the same role as the *oun* in 9:1. The ordinary Christian as well as the martyr is to follow the example of the Lord (vs. 1). Chapter 8 sets forth the principle; chapter 9 and chapter 10 are two applications of it. Martyrdom and the life of the brotherhood both spring from a proper understanding of the incarnate Christ, the pledge of our righteousness. The purpose of the exhortations in verses 2-3 is to encourage behavior that may prevent the name of God from being blasphemed among the Gentiles. The form that this encouragement takes is general and could apply both to the relations between Christians and to those involving also non-Christians.

no man.¹⁰ 2. "When you can *do good*, do not delay," ¹¹ "*because alms deliver from death.*" ¹² "*All of you* be subject *to one another,*" ¹³ "*maintaining your conduct among the Gentiles* irreproachable, *so that by your good works*" ¹⁴ you may receive praise, and the Lord may also *not be blasphemed* ¹⁵ because of you. 3. But "*woe to him through whom the name* of the Lord *is* blasphemed." ¹⁶ Therefore teach all men the sobriety in which you also walk.

X. Love of money: Valens (11:1-4a)

11 I am very unhappy on account of Valens, who was formerly made an elder among you, that he should so misunderstand the

¹² Tob. 4:11 (AB).
¹³ 1 Pet. 5:5 (cf. Eph. 5:21; Ign. Magn. 13:2).
¹⁴ 1 Pet. 2:12.   ¹⁵ Tit. 2:5.
¹⁶ Isa. 52:5; but the influence of a form of the verse like that in Ign. Trall. 1:2 has been felt.

Polycarp appears, however, to be stressing in particular the unfortunate results of moral failings within the community. That would explain (*a*) the close grammatical connection between the theme of being subject to one another and that of maintaining irreproachable conduct among the Gentiles and (*b*) the position of these verses in the letter: they may be regarded as preparing the way for the discussion of Valens, whose failing could well have caused offense to those outside the church and may well have threatened to become a public scandal (cf. 2:2) unless the members of the congregation exercised sobriety (cf. vs. 3; 11:4).

11:1-4a. Polycarp's expressions of grief over Valens and his wife (vss. 1, 4) enclose a general discussion concerning (*a*) love of money (vs. 1), (*b*) its dire consequences (vs. 2), (*c*) his confidence that these have never been realized in Philippi (vs. 3).

It deserves special notice that in verse 1 Polycarp immediately turns from the case of Valens to exhorting the congregation as a whole concerning love of money. This confirms our interpretation (see on 4:1) that he regards Valens' action as a sign of a profounder moral failing at Philippi. It is also to be noted that love of money brings men close to paganism (vs. 2)—not heresy. The connection between love of money and heresy is, as we have seen, less direct.

11:1. *Valens:* A familiar name in ancient Philippi (*CIL*, III, 633, 640, 690). *Love of money: Avaritia* translates *philargyria* in 2:2; 4:1; 4:3; 6:1. In 2:2 *pleonexia* is translated *concupiscentia*. The Greek, then, probably read *philargyria* here. *Pure and trustworthy: Casti veraces* (or *casti et veraces* in two MSS). *Castus* and *castitas* elsewhere translate *hagnos* and *hagneia* (4:2; 5:3). *Castus* ("chaste") suggests sex-

office given him. *I exhort you, then,*[1] *to abstain from*[2] *love of money*[3] *and to be pure and trustworthy. Abstain from all evil.*[4] 2. Indeed, how is he who cannot govern himself in these things to prescribe it to another?[5] If a man does not refrain from *love of money,*[6] he will be contaminated by *idolatry*[6] and will be judged

[1] See 9:1, n. 1. [2] See 2:2, n. 19.
[3] See 2:2, n. 22.
[4] See 2:2, n. 19 (the passage is most closely related to Job 2:3).
[5] Cf. 1 Tim. 3:5.
[6] Col. 3:5; Eph. 5:5; T. Jud. 19:1.

---

ual irregularity involving Valens and his wife (vs. 4a), but *hagnos* has a wider significance. It is basically a cultic word (cf. 1 Macc. 14:36), often used in our period figuratively of ethical purity (Clement, *Str.* 7.27.2; *Anthologia Palatina* 14.71,74; Porphyry, *De Abstinentia* 2.19). Lightfoot points out that a cultically oriented word is in place because of the connection drawn below between love of money and idolatry (vs. 2). He has also suggested, however, that the two adjectives may be alternate renderings (hence no *et*) of *eilikrineis* ("pure," "sincere"). 11:2. *Indeed, how . . . to another?*: Structurally and to some extent materially parallel to 1 Timothy 3:5. Similar motifs in Hellenistic paranesis (Dibelius pp. 43-44). *Autem,* like the Greek *de* or *dē*, is used in adding an emphatic question; hence, "but," "indeed." *Idolatry: Pleonexia* and *eidololatreia* linked in Colossians 3:5; Ephesians 5:5. *Philargyria* and *eidololatreia* linked in *T. Jud.* 19:1 (cf. Philo. *De Specialibus Legibus* 1.23). *Judge the world:* The quotation is chosen to drive home the spiritual bankruptcy of such a person; precisely, he is judged who ought to be judging. *As Paul teaches:* The formula seems to indicate that an apostle is not yet regarded as one who has written Scripture (Koester p. 113). In 3:1-3 Paul is certainly dealt with as an authority, his teachings are interpreted with the help of the sayings of the Lord, and his letters are regarded as valuable; but the value of Ignatius' letters is described in similar terms (13:2). See also 12:1, n. 12. (I remain unconvinced of the contrary by C. M. Nielsen, *ATR*, 47 [1965], 199-216.)

11:3. *Any such thing:* Polycarp is confident that no one in Philippi has ever gone so far in love of money as to be numbered with idolatrous Gentiles. *Perceived: Sensi,* which may translate *egnōn* (cf. Ign. Trall. 8:1) or *enoēsa* (cf. Ign. Smyrn. 1:1). The latter would imply that Polycarp himself had visited Philippi (Bauer). The parallel to Ignatius, Trallians 8:1 is striking, however, and speaks in favor of the former suggestion. *Who are (mentioned),* etc.: One of the most difficult passages in the letter. (a) According to H. Nolte and Lightfoot there is an allusion to 2 Corinthians 3:2-3, and the passage should be translated: "who were [*estis* for the temporally neutral *tois ousin*] his letters in the beginning." The allusion, however, would be obscure, especially since

as though he were one of the Gentiles [7] who *"know not the judgment of the Lord."* [8] *Or do we not know that the saints will judge the world,"* [9] as Paul teaches? 3. But *I have not perceived or heard of any such thing among you,*[10] in whose midst the blessed Paul labored and who are (mentioned) in the beginning of his letter. For of you he *boasts in all the churches* [11] which alone at that time *knew God;* [12] for we had not yet known him. 4a. I am exceedingly unhappy, then, on account of that man and his wife; to whom may *the Lord give* true *repentance!* [13]

[7] Cf. Matt. 18:17 (Ezek. 20:32). [8] Jer. 5:4.
[9] 1 Cor. 6:2. [10] Ign. Trall. 8:1.
[11] 2 Thess. 1:4. [12] Gal. 4:9. [13] 2 Tim. 2:25.

Paul refers to the Corinthians as his "letter" (sing.). (*b*) Zahn suggests that the Greek read "in the beginning of his apostolate" (cf. Gal. 2:8), drawing attention to the confusion between the readings *apostello* and *epistello* in 1 Samuel 5:8; Nehemiah 12:19; Acts 21:25. (*c*) G. Krüger suggests "in the beginning of the *gospel*" on the strength of 1 Clement 47:2. (*d*) A. Hilgenfeld accepts the reading of one MS—"in the beginning of the church." (*e*) T. Smith has persuaded Bauer and others that *laudati* ought to be supplied—"who were praised in the beginning of his letter." He regarded this as a reference to Philippians 1:3-11. Bauer throws out the tenuous suggestion that the allusion to 2 Thessalonians 1:4 may have been consciously applied to the Philippians because of the supposed unity of the Macedonian congregations (cf. 2 Cor. 8:1-2). The solution, however, presupposes a very unusual textual error. (*f*) Harnack accepted the emendation of Smith but thinks that originally there must have been some reference to the Philippians in 2 Thessalonians, since it is alluded to in the following sentence. (*g*) Ed. Schweizer (*ThZ*, 1 [1945], 90-98) has gone further and suggested that 2 Thessalonians was originally written to Philippi (see also on 3:2). He admits the possibility that Polycarp quoted 2 Thessalonians 1:4 thinking it had come from Philippians (cf. the confusion in Tertullian, *Scorpiace* 13), but he prefers to think that the quotation of the passage makes sense only if the letter were originally sent to Philippi. He thinks that Smith's emendation is the best, but is not convinced that any is needed (he supplies "mentioned"). The following objections may be urged against this thesis: (*a*) Note that Paul's Philippians is ignored also in 3:2-3 despite Polycarp's reference to the apostle's "letters" to Philippi. (*b*) The reference here to "his letter [to you?]" suggests, if anything, knowledge of only one letter to Philippi. (*c*) The allusion to 2 Thessalonians 1:4 is only an allusion, and we have seen how freely Polycarp gives new application to older materials. A passage like Philippians 4:15-16 may well have been interpreted as special commendation of the Philippians in all the churches.

XI. Sobriety "in this thing" (11:4b–12:1)

4b. *Therefore* you too *be sober*[1] in this matter; *"and do not consider such people as enemies,"*[2] but *bring them back as weak and erring*[3] *members*[4] *"that you may preserve your body in its entirety."*[5] *For by doing this*[6] *you build up one another.*[7] 12 For

[1] Pet. 4:7.
[3] See 6:1, n. 44.
[5] 1 Clem. 37:5.
[7] 1 Thess. 5:11; 1 Cor. 14:4, 26.

[2] 2 Thess. 3:15.
[4] 1 Cor. 12:12, etc.
[6] 1 Tim. 4:16.

And this suggests that if any emendation is required, one reflecting Philippians 4:15 ("in the beginning of the gospel") is more likely to be correct; the difference between *euaggeliou* and *epistolēs* in Greek uncials is perhaps not too great to have caused error. (*d*) That there is no emphasis on the quotation is suggested by the following observations: Polycarp is extolling the absence of "any such thing" among the Philippians; but it is also an indirect exhortation to persevere in faithfulness and to preserve it unbroken. Here the emphasis is on the sheer fact of their belonging to the first Christian communities, unlike the Smyrnaeans ("we") who were not yet Christians in apostolic times (the first reference to churches in Smyrna is in Rev. 2:8). It is the very fact that Paul labored in Philippi (and wrote to them?) that is important (consequently the colorlessness of the *qui estis* clause?). The theme, then, is not so much one of praise involving reference to a particular passage, but one of exhortation based on appeals to the ancient heritage of the church in Philippi (as in 3:2). The *etenim* clause, then, need not be taken to refer exclusively to the immediately preceding clause; and there is no need to supply a *laudati* there. Insufficient attention has been given to the train of thought suggested particularly by the clause "for we had not yet known him." All this fits in with Polycarp's concern that Valens be reinstated to prevent a break in the tradition of faithfulness at Philippi.

11:4b–12:1. The Philippians are urged to deal moderately with Valens (11:4b). They are reminded of biblical passages which underscore the importance of such moderation (12:1).

The section 11:4b–12:1 forms a unit distinct in content from what precedes and what follows. Its unity has not been recognized partly because of the ambiguous second sentence of 12:1 (see below). The *enim* of the first sentence of 12:1 is more than a simple particle of transition. The function of the OT passages quoted is to underscore the necessity of dealing kindly with Valens and his wife. The section brings to fulfillment the hints thrown out in 2:2-3 and 6:2.

11:4b. *Weak: pathētos* (cf. Plutarch, *Pelopidas* 16); possibly a medical metaphor—"diseased" (LSJ, 1285). 12:1. *But that has not been left to me* (or: "But the initiative in this matter is not mine").

I am confident that [8] *you are well trained in the sacred writings;* [9] *and nothing is hid from you.*[10] *But that has not been left to me; only, as it is said in these Scriptures, "be angry and do not sin,"* [11] *and "let not the sun set upon your wrath."* [12] *Blessed is he* [13] *who remembers* [9] *(this); which I am confident is the case with you.*[14]

XII. The prayer (12:2-3)

2. Now may *the God and Father of our Lord Jesus Christ,*[1] *and the eternal high priest* [2] *himself, the Son of God,*[3] *Jesus Christ,*[4]

---

[8] Rom. 8:38; 2 Tim. 1:5.
[10] Ign. Eph. 14:1.
[11] Ps. 4:5 quoted in Eph. 4:26.
[12] Eph. 4:26. Probably cited from memory and mistakenly taken to be from the OT because of the link in Ephesians with Ps. 4:5 (see n. 11). There is a similar confusion in 1 Tim. 5:18.
[13] Rev. 1:3; 22:7.
[14] 2 Tim. 1:5; Ign. Trall. 3:2.

[9] 1 Clem. 53:1.

[1] Rom. 15:6; Eph. 1:3; 1 Pet. 1:3; 2 Cor. 1:3.
[2] Heb. 6:20 (cf. 1 Clem. 36:1; Ign. Philad. 9:1).
[3] Heb. 7:3.   [4] 2 Cor. 1:19.

The more natural translation is: "That [knowledge of Scripture], however, has not been granted me." Such humility would scarcely be beyond the spiritual capacities of Polycarp. Yet it seems out of place here. Polycarp was a bishop and had been a Christian from his youth (Mart. Polyc. 9:3). The language here (*mihi non est concessum—* that is, *emoi de ouk epitrepetai*) is similar to that in 3:1 (*ouk emautō epitrepsas:* "not on my own initiative"), where diffidence is not to be taken as an admission of inferiority to the Philippians. The Philippians are to edify themselves (11:4b). They know the OT. To instruct them in it is not Polycarp's task. All he will permit himself to do (*modo*) is to draw attention to a few key verses from the Bible. The punctuation in the translation reflects this understanding of the passage.

12:2-3. The prayer addressed to God and Christ on behalf of Christians consists of two petitions: (1) that God edify the Philippians, and (2) that he give them and future believing generations a place among the saints (vs. 2). There follow exhortations to pray for (*a*) political authorities, (*b*) persecutors, and (*c*) heretics.

The prayer reflects the concerns of the letter: edification (3:2; 11:4; 13:2), faith (1:2; 4:2; 9:2; 13:2), truth (2:1; 3:2; 4:2; 5:2; 10:1), gentleness (10:1), freedom from anger (12:1), endurance (9:1; 13:2), long-suffering and forbearance (cf. 6:1-2; 11:4–12:1), purity (5:3; 11:1). The view of the saints as a sort of church above in glory is in harmony with other sentiments of Polycarp (9:2; 11:2). The

build you up in *faith and truth* [5] and *in all gentleness* [6] and *without anger* [7] and in *patience* and in *long-suffering* [8] and *forbearance* [9] and *purity;* [10] and may he give to you *a lot and portion* [11] with *his saints,*[12] and to us along with you, and to *all men who are under heaven* [13] *who will believe in* [14] *our Lord Jesus Christ* [15] and in his *Father who raised him from the dead.*[16] 3. "*Pray for all the saints.*" [17] Pray also *for kings* [18] and *powers* and *princes* [19] and

[5] 1 Clem. 60:4; 1 Tim. 2:7.
[6] Ign. Philad. 1:2 (see 10:1 above, n. 9).
[7] 1 Tim. 2:8.   [8] Rom. 2:4.   [9] 2 Cor. 1:6.
[10] 1 Tim. 4:12; 5:2; Ign. Eph. 10:3.
[11] Col. 1:12; Acts 8:21; 26:18; cf. Deut. 12:12; 14:26, 28; Josh. 14:3-4.
[12] Col. 1:12; Eph. 1:18 (see n. 11).
[13] Col. 1:23; Acts 2:5.
[14] 1 Tim. 1:16; 1 Clem. 42:4.   [15] Acts 11:17.
[16] Gal. 1:1 (cf. Col. 2:12; 1 Pet. 1:21).
[17] Eph. 6:18.   [18] 1 Tim. 2:1-2.
[19] Rom. 13:1 ff. (cf. 1 Clem. 60:4; 61:1-3).

emphasis on the resurrection of Christ is found earlier in the letter (2:1, etc.). The reference to Christ as eternal high priest alone stands out; it is a common theme in our period (see n. 2) and also occurs in the prayer of Polycarp in the Martyrdom of Polycarp 14:3.

The catholic concern of Polycarp is manifest in prayer for all men (see nn. 17-19; cf. Ign. Eph. 10:1). It is similarly expressed again in the Martyrdom of Polycarp 5:1 and is shown to be part of the traditional teaching of the Church in the same document (10:2).

12:2. *Our Lord Jesus Christ:* According to four MSS, "our Lord and God Jesus Christ" (cf. John 20:28; Ign. Eph. 7:2; 19:3). Christ is regularly called simply "our Lord" (1:1; 1:2; 2:1; 6:3) or "the Lord" (6:2, 3; 7:2; 10:1) by Polycarp. *Saints:* Of the Christians who are with the Lord (cf. Origen, *PG*, XI, 448b; Athanasius, *PG*, XXVII, 497d; Gregory of Nyssa, *PG*, XLVI, 12a). They do not form a special group nor is there any idea of an exterior cult connected with the term (Delehaye, *Sanctus*, 30). We are still close to the language of the NT (see n. 12). **12:3.** *For kings:* The term "king" was regularly used in Greek for the Roman emperor (LSJ, 309; it is most artificial to suggest that the plural reflects a time when there were coemperors). There was Jewish precedent for such a prayer (2 Esdr. 6:9-10; Baruch 1:11; Ps.-Aristeas 45; 1 Macc. 7:33; Josephus, *Bell.* 2.197, 409; Philo, *Legatio* 157, 317; *In Flaccum* 49; *Pirke Abot* 3.2). The NT (Rom. 13:1 ff.; 1 Pet. 2:13-14, 17; Tit. 3:1) and the early Church (Justin, *Apol.* 1.17.3; Theophilus, *Ad Autol* 1.11; Tertullian, *Apology* 30, 39; Acts of Cyprian 2) take it for granted. *The enemies of the cross:* In light of 7:1, probably a reference to Docetists.

"for *those who persecute* and *hate you*"[20] and for the *enemies of the cross*,[21] that *your fruit may be plain to all men*,[22] "that you may *be perfect*"[20] *in him*.[23]

XIII. The letters of Ignatius (13:1-2)

13 * Both you and Ignatius write me to have your letter taken along by anyone who is going to Syria. This I shall do if I have a

[20] Matt. 5:44, 48: "Love your enemies [Byz D Lat (cf. Luke 6:27-28) add: "bless those who curse you, do good to those who *hate you*"] and *pray for* those who persecute you. . . . You shall be perfect" (cf. Did. 1:3-4). Direct dependence on Matthew (with contamination from Luke) in this passage is indicated by the fact that the connection of themes in Matt. 5:44 and 5:48 has the marks of a Matthean construction (Koester pp. 119–120).
[21] Phil. 3:18.
[22] Tit. 3:14; 1 Tim. 4:15.
[23] Col. 2:10 (where "in him" means "in Christ").

* At this point a portion of the Greek text (preserved by Eusebius) resumes.

13:1–2. This is a reply to the Philippians' request (1) that Smyrna forward their letter to Ignatius' congregation in Syria and (2) that copies of the letters of Ignatius be sent to Philippi. There follows a brief eulogy of the letters and a request that any news concerning Ignatius and those with him be sent on to Smyrna.

The notes and comments below explore Harrison's thesis that chapters 1–12 and 13–14 form two separate letters. In order to establish this view, Harrison makes much of the "urgency" of Ignatius' and the Philippians' requests and the alacrity of Polycarp in responding to their letter. Only in this way can he outflank the argument that Polycarp may have "assumed" that Ignatius was dead without really knowing whether he was or not. Sufficient time would not have elapsed.

We cannot analyze Ignatius' remarks in detail. Harrison suggests that by "peace" in Antioch (e.g., Smyrn. 11:1-3) he was referring not to cessation of persecution but of factional strife. Hence the "urgent" request to send ambassadors. We may note, however, that *eirēneuein* in 4 Maccabees 18:4—a document linked with Ignatius in many ways (O. Perler, *Rivista di Archeologia Cristiana* 25 [1949], 47-72)—is used of peace after persecution (note also that the related images of "fair weather" and the "harbor" are also employed in 4 Macc. 7:1-3; 13:6-7). In any event, it seems to me that the intensity of Ignatius' tone is rooted in the cosmic significance which he accords his own death, the peace in the church, and the movement of ambassadors. I doubt that the term "urgency" accurately describes the tone of his language.

Harrison further claims that it is inconceivable that Polycarp would have waited so long in answering the requests of the Philippians to be

convenient opportunity—either myself or someone whom I send
as ambassador[1] for you as well as me. 2. We are sending you at
your request the letters of Ignatius which he sent to us and any

[1] Ign. Philad. 10:1.   [2] See 3:2, n. 10.

---

able to "assume" that Ignatius had been martyred. He has argued (pp.
107-117) that it would take a minimum of from six to seven weeks for
Ignatius to get to Rome from Philippi. But the Philippians' letter, if
sent off immediately, would take only a week to get to Polycarp. No
doubt Polycarp would reply soon; and that reply is chapters 13-14 of
our letter; in it he does not yet know whether Ignatius has been
martyred.

But a rather longer time may have been involved in the exchange of
letters between the Philippians and Polycarp. We must give the Philippians time to compose (in addition to a brief note) at least a letter of
congratulations to the church in Antioch (and, on our theory, a letter
to Polycarp discussing their own problems). We need not assume that
the Philippians would have rushed to get their messenger to Smyrna
before the Smyrnaean messenger left for Antioch (Harrison pp. 117-
118); for if Ignatius told them that Polycarp was supposed to be in
charge of collecting a number of letters to take to Antioch (Ign.
Polyc. 7-8), they would have been aware that this would take time—
especially if, as is possible (Bauer p. 281), the churches *emprosthen*
which Polycarp was to contact lay before Ignatius on his way to
Rome. Following Harrison's own calculations (pp. 111-112), from
seven to fourteen days must be allowed for a trip between Philippi and
Smyrna; we cannot assume that a messenger would necessarily have
made it in the shortest possible time. One must also allow Polycarp
time to get together copies of Ignatius' letters (we need not assume
that he had extra copies ready). If he wrote also chapters 1-12 at this
time, he must be given time for that. In any event, he would write
chapter 13 with the knowledge that it would take another seven to
fourteen days for his letter to be read by the Philippians; the epistolary
aorists show the perspective from which men usually wrote letters; he
may well have assumed that by that time Ignatius would have met his
fate. Messengers may not always have been immediately available.
Finally, the matter of Polycarp's "slower-moving disposition" (cf. Ign.
Polyc. 3:2) cannot be brushed so lightly aside (Harrison pp. 126-
128).

Harrison pp. 132, 163-165 also argues that because chapters 1-12
are filled with echoes from Ignatius' writings, Polycarp must be given
time to absorb them. But chapters 13-14, as Harrison also grants,
have a number of echoes of Ignatian language, and the echoes in
chapters 1-12 are in no case so clear that we felt constrained to
enclose them in quotation marks. Nor can we make too much of
Polycarp's dependence on the written Gospels, Paul, and a number of

others which we possess. They are attached to this letter. *You will be able* [2] *to benefit* [3] *greatly from them. For they deal with faith*

[3] Cf. 2 Tim. 3:16 (*ōphelimos*).

---

other NT works (and also 1 Clement) in chapters 1-12. The subject matter of chapters 13-14 is sufficient explanation of the relative paucity of allusions there. And we have no reason to doubt that such documents were available to others had they wanted to use them. Thus even if, as Koester maintains, Polycarp was the first whom we know to make use of the written Gospels, it is more likely that we are dealing with a personal bent rather than with evidence of a new—that is, later—attitude in the Church as a whole to NT writings.

The opinion of some older scholars that chapter 13 is not genuine has been revived recently by Grégoire (*Persécutions*, 102-104). He regards Polycarp's letter as interpolated for the sake of lending authenticity to the Ignatian corpus, which he places late in the second century. But surely the whole of Polycarp's letter would have been placed later had it not been for Irenaeus' clear witness to it (*Adv. haer.* 3.3.4). Grégoire's argument resorts too quickly to a theory of interpolation and depends too much on a reconstruction of the persecutions in the second century, which is questionable on many grounds.

13:1. *Both you and Ignatius:* A similar request but of a more general nature is to be found in Ignatius' letter to Polycarp (7:2; 8:1). There is no difficulty in imagining that Polycarp automatically gave it this particular application, especially under the influence of the letter from the Philippians. We need not assume that this letter was accompanied by further (urgent) instructions from Ignatius. *Anyone who* (*ean tis*) . . . *if* (*ean*): The more vivid expectation of the fulfillment of the condition introduced by *ean* may lead here as elsewhere (John 12:32; Tob. 4:3) to a shift in meaning best represented by the English "when" (Harrison p. 93, n. 2). This interpretation, however, lends little support to Harrison's emphasis on the urgency of the request. It makes Polycarp's attitude somewhat more definite, but that is all. There is still a possibility that the "if" ought to be retained in its normal sense. Harrison p. 93, n. 2, to be sure, complains that "the Philippians will not have sent their messenger 300 miles on the off-chance that Polycarp might perhaps be sending his messenger to Antioch." But that already presupposes Harrison's conclusions that they did not have other serious questions to be dealt with—the problem of heresy and the problem of Valens' sin. That Polycarp would turn Ignatius' strong recommendations (Ign. Polyc. 7:2; 8:1) into a condition is not outside the range of possibilities. Nor is the condition best represented by the phrase "on the off-chance that"; *ean* with the subject means "if, as is to be expected" (B-D, 190). Other action was possible; the Smyrnaeans could have sent a messenger part way as had the Philippians. Harrison p. 93 is on firmer ground when he suggests

and *endurance*[4] and all the *edification*[5] *which belongs to*[6] our Lord.† And let us know anything more certain which you learn about Ignatius himself and those with him.

[4] 2 Thess. 1:4; Jas. 1:3 (cf. Ign. Polyc. 6:2; Eph. 3:1; 1 Clem. 62:2; 64).
[5] Rom. 15:2 (14:23, "faith"; 15:2, "edification"; 15:4, "endurance").
[6] Ign. Polyc. 7:3 (cf. Ign. Philad. 1:1).
† The Greek fragment from Eusebius ends at this point.

that the force of the second sentence may be, "I will do it myself, if I can find or make suitable opportunity; otherwise I will certainly send someone else." That "certainly" may be too strong; in any event, the interpretation suggests definite purpose rather than urgency. *Convenient opportunity:* Harrison p. 79 represents this phrase by "on the first opportunity" or p. 119 "in due course, meaning, at the earliest possible moment." In this way he underscores the urgency of the request. But the adjective "convenient" or "favorable" does not suggest great haste. It is best taken in the normal sense that it has in a similar expression in Diodorus Siculus 5.57.4. (The peculiar "biblical" sense of the phrase in Ps. 31:6 does not seem to play a role here.) *Myself:* Ignatius had not contemplated this possibility (Ign. Polyc. 7:2; Smyrn. 11:2), but other churches had sent their bishops (Ign. Philad. 10:2). **13:2.** *At your request:* The verb may mean "as requested" or "as instructed" (Harrison p. 320). But it is difficult to read much greater urgency into the second translation. *Any others:* The Greek construction makes it clear that this was part of the Philippians' request. *Those with him:* Zosimus, Rufus (9:1) and/or Philo, Rheus Agathopus (Ign. Philad. 11:1; Smyrn. 10:1). The last sentence in verse 2 (unfortunately retained only in Latin) is a key element in Harrison's thesis. This statement implies that Polycarp does not know about the fate of Ignatius and his companions, whereas a clear reference to their death is to be found in 9:1 (though we have argued above that the latter is vaguer than commentators assume). Lightfoot suggested that the original of *qui cum eo sunt* was *tois syn autō* (the *tois syn autō* of the inscription is translated *qui cum eo sunt*) and that this is temporally neutral. It may mean, therefore, "who were with him." Polycarp is aware of Ignatius' death (cf. 9:1), but full particulars (*certius*) have not yet arrived. This is very artificial even if the retranslation is correct (Harrison pp. 137-140). It is more likely that the *qui cum eo sunt* refers to the living—*or, more precisely, to those still most vividly remembered as alive;* if so, Polycarp writes (both here and in 9:1) before the news of Ignatius' death had arrived but after "it might reasonably be held that he had been martyred" (A. C. Headlam, *Church Quarterly Review* 141 [1945], 7). Our own interpretation of 9:1-2 may be taken to favor this suggestion. In any event, the apparently fresh memory of the martyrs in 1:1 should prevent us from driving too deep a wedge between 9:1 and 13:1.

XIV. Conclusion (14:1)

14 *I am writing these things to you by* [1] Crescens, whom I have recommended *to you* in the past and now recommend [2] again. For he has *walked among us blamelessly;* [3] and *I believe that he did so also among you.*[4] And you may consider his sister recommended when she comes to you. *Farewell* in our Lord Jesus Christ *in grace,*[5] you and all yours. Amen.

[1] Ign. Rom. 10:1, 3.   [2] Rom. 16:1.   [3] 1 Clem. 63:3.
[4] See 12:1, n. 14.   [5] Ign. Smyrn. 13:2.

14:1. Two elements make up the concluding remarks: (1) commendation of Crescens and his sister and (2) the complimentary close.

Crescens: For the name see 2 Timothy 4:10; *CIL,* III, 633 (Philippi). *By Crescens:* The *dia* indicates that Crescens was the bearer of the letter (cf. Ign. Rom. 10:1; Philad. 11:2; Smyrn. 12:1) and may have had something to do with the drawing up of the document (cf. Eusebius, *H.E.* 4.23.11). If the theory of two letters is accepted, the reference to a previous commendation of Crescens may indicate that he carried the note to which Ignatius' letters were appended (13:1-2); if so, this chapter 14 would belong to the longer later letter (Kleist, *ACW,* VI, 196; cf. Harrison p. 206). That would presuppose a close relation between the two letters. *In the past:* The Latin actually reads *in praesenti,* "at present," "now." The antithesis with *nunc,* "now," makes that impossible. Lightfoot suggests that *in praesenti* was an unfortunate translation of *arti,* which means both "now" and "just now" (with clear reference to the past in Plato, *Meno* 89c and elsewhere). Zahn's explanation—the original *eis to paron* really meant "until the present" (that is, at every opportunity)—is forced (for *eis* like *pros* with *to paron* has to do with the present or with one's intentions in present circumstances; cf. Philo, *De Gigantibus* 56, 67). Bauer p. 298 suggests that it had something to do with Polycarp being "present" in Philippi (cf. 11:3); along this line Harrison p. 328 accepts the reading *praesentem olim*—that is, *paronta arti.* But that is very speculative. It may be that the translator (or a Greek scribe) in reading ENTOIPARELTHONTI ("in the past"; cf. Aristotle, *Physics* 218a 9 and Basil, *Ad Adolescentes* 10.30 for *to parelthon* of the "past") missed three (Greek) letters (ELTH) and saw ENTOIPARONTI ("in the present"). *And I believe that he did:* The form of the expression is like that in 2 Timothy 1:5, where the verb is not expressed. In both cases we are dealing with an assurance that what is asserted is in fact a reality. But it is impossible to tell here whether we are dealing with an opinion concerning the past or the (hoped for) future behavior of Crescens. The fact of a past commendation makes a past stay of Crescens at Philippi probable; reference to his past behavior, then, is more probable.

SELECTED BIBLIOGRAPHY

(Books or articles marked * are usually cited only by the author's name)

* BAUER, W., *Die apostolischen Väter* (*Handbuch zum Neuen Testament*). Tübingen, 1923.
——, *Rechtgläubigkeit und Ketzerei im ältesten Christentum* (*Beiträge zur historischen Theologie*, Vol. X). Tübingen, 1934.
CADOUX, C. J., "Polycarp's Two Epistles to the Philippians, by P. N. Harrison," *Journal of Theological Studies* 38 (1937), 267-270.
CAMPENHAUSEN, H. F. VON, *Die Idee des Martyriums in der alten Kirche*. Göttingen, 1936.
——, *Polykarp von Smyrna und die Pastoralbriefe* (*Sitzungsberichte der Heidelberger Akademie der Wissenschaften: Philosophisch-historische Klasse*, Jahrgang 1951, 2. Abteilung). Heidelberg, 1951. (Abbreviation: SHA, 1951.)
DAHL, N. A., "Der Erstgeborene Satans und der Vater des Teufels (Polyk. 7:1 und Joh. 8:44)," in *Apophoreta: Festschrift für Ernst Haenchen* (Berlin, 1964), 70-84.
DELEHAYE, H., *Sanctus: Essai sur le culte des saints dans l'antiquité* (*Subsidia Hagiographica*, Vol. XVII). Brussels, 1927.
*DIBELIUS, M., *Die Pastoralbriefe* (*Handbuch zum Neuen Testament*, Vol. XIII). 3d ed. rev. H. Conzelmann. Tübingen, 1955.
GRÉGOIRE, H., et al., *Les persécutions dans l'empire Romain* (*Académie royale de Belgique: classe des lettres et des sciences morales et politiques: mémoires*, 1st ed., Vol. XLVI/1; 2d ed. rev., Vol. LVI/5). Brussels, 1951, 1964.
*HARNACK, A. VON, *Marcion: Das Evangelium vom fremden Gott*. Darmstadt, 1960.
*HARRISON, P. N., *Polycarp's Two Epistles to the Philippians*. Cambridge, Eng., 1936.
KLEIST, J. A., *The Didache, The Epistle of Barnabas, The Epistles and the Martyrdom of St. Polycarp, The Fragments of Papias, The Epistle to Diognetus* (*Ancient Christian Writers*, Vol. VI). Westminster, Md., 1961. (Abbreviation: ACW, VI.)
*KOESTER, H., *Synoptische Überlieferungen bei den Apostolischen Vätern* (*Texte und Untersuchungen*, 65). Berlin, 1957.
*LAMPE, G. W. H. (ed.), *A Patristic Greek Lexicon*. Oxford, 1961-.
*LIGHTFOOT, J. B., *The Apostolic Fathers, Part II: S. Ignatius, S. Polycarp*. 3 vols. 2d ed. rev. London, 1889.
MEINHOLD, P., "Polycarpos," in *Paulys Realencyclopädie der classischen Altertumswissenschaft*, ed. G. Wissowa and W. Kroll, XXI/2 (Stuttgart, 1952), 1662-1693. (Abbreviation: PWK, XXI.)

The *New Testament in the Apostolic Fathers by a Committee of the Oxford Society of Historical Theology*. Oxford, 1905.

PUECH, H.-C., "P. N. Harrison, Polycarp's Two Epistles to the Philippians," *Revue de l'histoire des religions* 119 (1939), 96-102.

SCHWEIZER, ED., "Der zweite Thessalonickerbrief ein Philipperbrief?" *Theologische Zeitschrift* 1 (1945), 90-105.

*TORRANCE, T. F., *The Doctrine of Grace in the Apostolic Fathers*. Grand Rapids, Mich., 1948.

*VÖLTER, D., *Die Apostolischen Väter, neu untersucht*, Vol. II/2: *Polycarp und Ignatius und die ihnen zugeschriebenen Briefe*. Leiden, 1910.

ZAHN, TH., *Ignatius von Antiochien*. Gotha, 1873.

———, *Ignatii et Polycarpi Epistulae, Martyria, Fragmenta* (*Patrum Apostolicorum Opera*, Vol. II). 3d ed. Leipzig, 1876.

———, *Introduction to the New Testament*. 3 vols. New York, 1909.

THE MARTYRDOM
OF POLYCARP

THE MARTYRDOM OF POLYCARP

Introduction

The Martyrdom of Polycarp is an entirely different type of document from Polycarp to the Philippians despite the epistolary form. It is the first of the martyr acts from the early Church. Yet the martyr as a religious type, manifested in greater or lesser measure in the Maccabean literature, the New Testament, and figures such as Ignatius, was known to the congregation in Smyrna and controlled the account of the martyrdom of their bishop. There is, in fact, a framework which, although it does not necessarily create fiction, profoundly interpenetrates the story of the martyrdom.

The concentration of much of Roman Catholic work on the historicity of martyr acts (cf. H. Delehaye, *The Legends of the Saints* [New York, 1962]) is connected especially with a concern to minimize the supposed influence of non-Christian religious structures on these acts. The assumption seems to be that historicity precludes significant borrowing and that structural analogies between pagan religiosity and the early Church's understanding of sainthood are no longer suspect if no genealogical connection can be demonstrated. It is symptomatic that the basic task of the modern investigator is interpreted in terms of purifying the tradition of "excesses and extravagances" and of identifying that which is historically trustworthy. The concern is determined in part by a dogmatic emphasis rooted in the Bible's teaching on the unity of God and, I suspect, by a certain rationalism which is offended by undisciplined products of the religious imagination. In any event, such "excesses" or "aberrations" are, as the terms imply, not of the essence, and the scholar can show that there is an underlying continuity of Christian truth also in the hagiographical tradition.

It is more typical of Protestant work on the martyr acts to stress the discontinuity between the biblical faith and the early Church's understanding of sainthood. When H. von Campenhausen in *Die Idee des Martyriums in der alten Kirche* finds a "falling away" from New Testament insights in the early Church, sees in Augustine the great exception to the rule, and credits Luther with the decisive recovery of a biblical perspective on martyrdom, we recognize the outlines of a now-classical Protestant interpretation of the history of dogma.

Much may be learned from both approaches; but there is a tendency in either case to burden the study of the early Church with artificial issues. The significance of the figure of the martyr as a religious type is filled out with the help of numerous motifs from Graeco-Roman and Jewish piety, as we shall see. At the same time, fundamental biblical motifs—such as the emphasis on the divine will and election and God's glory (20:1)—are also operative. Here too, as in the thinking of the early Greek church generally, we find a subtle blend of religious and theological perspectives which must be allowed to speak its own idiom.

What gives coherence to the figure of the martyr as a religious type is not easy to say. It has occurred to me that the image of the "birthday" (18:3) may be of greater importance than would appear at first sight. Is not martyrdom a sort of higher initiation into a new form of existence? The transformation of the martyr (2:2-3; cf. 12:1; 15:2), the martyr's possession of preternatural powers (13:2; cf. 18:1-3), the image of sacrifice (14:1-2), and the very theme of the imitation of Christ (1:1-2; 19:1) are not out of harmony with such an interpretation. It is perhaps significant religiously (as well as exegetically; cf. Mark 10:38-39) that martyrdom and baptism were connected at an early period (Origen, *Commentary on Matthew* 16.6; *Exhortation to Martyrdom* 30). That such an initiation depends on God's will and favor and tends ultimately to his glory (2:1; 20:1) links martyrdom with the Church's awareness of a destiny also in the arena of history. The early connection between martyrdom and witness to the reality of Christ's passion (see p. 24) points in the same direction.

The Martyrdom of Polycarp claims to be the work of eyewitnesses (15:1) written within a year of the event (18:3). There appears to be no good reason to deny these claims. But it does seem to me that von Campenhausen (*SHA*, 1957, No. 3) is right in regarding the document as interpolated. I have found it necessary to qualify his analysis, especially in reference to the beginning and ending of the book, but in many ways I have found his arguments persuasive. As for the date of Polycarp's martyrdom, the evidence seems to point to a time between, say, A.D. 155 and 160. Greater precision is impossible (see p. 78).

The following are the Greek manuscripts of the Martyrdom of Polycarp: b h m p v c. The fragment edited by Papadopulos is of no real value. Some good readings are preserved in a tenth-eleventh-century encomium of Polycarp attributed to Chrysostom. Eusebius carefully paraphrases the section 2:2–7:3 (in *H.E.* 4.15. 4-14) and quotes the inscription, 1:1a, and 8:1–19:1a (in *H.E.* 4.15.3, 15-45). Of the versions, the Latin has some independent value. The Armenian, Syriac, and Coptic are derived from the text of Eusebius (H. Müller's high evaluation of the Armenian was misguided; see Reuning pp. 4-6). The manuscript m is generally regarded as the best (then b and p); an agreement between m and Eusebius, especially when supported by b and p, may be regarded as decisive; the value of m, however, ought not to be overestimated, as it was by Schwartz in *De Pionio et Polycarpo*. Our translation follows essentially the reconstruction of the text by Karl Bihlmeyer, *Die apostolischen Vaeter: Neubearbeitung der Funkschen Ausgabe*, rev. Wilhelm Schneemelcher, I (Tübingen: J. C. B. Mohr [Paul Siebeck], 1956), 120-132. Limitations of space have not permitted adequate discussion of the textual problems in the commentary.

Outline

Salutation (Inscription)
I. Martyrdom in accord with the gospel (1:1-2)
II. The noble martyrs of Christ (2:1-4)
III. Germanicus (3:1-2)
IV. Quintus (4:1)
V. Polycarp's withdrawal (5:1-2)
VI. Polycarp's arrest (6:1–7:3)
VII. On the way (8:1-3)
VIII. Polycarp's trial (9:1–11:2)
IX. The martyrdom of Polycarp: Preliminaries (12:1–13:3)
X. The martyrdom of Polycarp: The prayer (14:1-3)
XI. The martyrdom of Polycarp: The burning (15:1–16:2)
XII. The relics of Polycarp (17:1–18:3)
XIII. Conclusion (19:1–20:2)
Appendix I (21:1)
Appendix II (22:1)
Appendix IIIA (22:2)
Appendix IIIB (22:3)
Appendix IV: The Moscow epilogue

The Martyrdom of Polycarp

Translation and Commentary

Salutation (Inscription)

The church of God sojourning at Smyrna to the church of God sojourning in Philomelium and to all the communities of the holy and universal church sojourning in every place; mercy, peace, and love of God the Father and our Lord Jesus Christ be multiplied.

I. Martyrdom in accord with the gospel (1:1-2)

1 We are writing to you, brethren, an account of those martyred, especially the blessed Polycarp, who brought the persecu-

---

Salutation. For the form and content of the salutation see Polycarp to the Philippians, inscr.; 1 Clement, inscr.; 1 Corinthians 1:2 (cf. Eusebius, *H.E.* 4.23.5); Jude 2. *Smyrna:* For the city and its history see *Ancient Smyrna*, the exhaustive study by Cadoux. *Philomelium:* A city in Phrygia Paroreios about fifteen miles northeast of Pisidian Antioch but separated from it by a mountain range (Strabo, *Geographia* 12.8.14; Ptolemy, *Geographia* 5.2.17; Pliny, *Nat. hist.* 5.25). Though rather small, it was not without importance (Cicero, *Ad Familiares* 3.8, 15.4). *Communities . . . sojourning:* The two words represent one Greek word—*paroikiai*. This noun is related to the verb "sojourn." Thus it refers to the separated "parishes" of the universal Church (BAG, 634; cf. Eusebius, *H.E.* 4.23.5; 5.18.9; 5.25.14-17). Although the biblical background to the idea is probably fundamental (cf. Polyc. Phil. inscr.), an element of Stoic-Platonic cosmopolitanism may also be presupposed (cf. Diog. 5–6). *Universal:* The early sense of the term *katholikos* (cf. Ign. Smyrn. 8:2). Eusebius (*H.E.* 4.15.3) reads "holy universal church." *In every place:* Contrast 20:1 (cf. 1 Cor. 1:2).

1:1-2. In his paraphrase of the Martyrdom of Polycarp, Eusebius passes over the imitation theme (1:1a-2:1) here and elsewhere (*H.E.* 4.15.3-4). This has led H. Müller and following him von Campenhausen (*SHA*, 1957, No. 3) to suggest that the imitation theme was the main door through which interpolations entered the book. There is

tion to an end as though putting a seal upon it through his martyrdom. For all that preceded it, we dare say, took place that the Lord might show us again martyrdom in accord with the gospel.

---

some truth in this, as we shall see, but I am not convinced that we have an interpolation in 1:1a–2:1.

The imitation theme in connection with suffering and martyrdom is common in the early Church (Delehaye, *Genres*, 17-21; Reuning pp. 10-11; cf. Polyc. Phil. 8:2) and goes back to the NT (Acts 7:59-60; cf. Eusebius *H.E.* 2.23.4-18). But not only does von Campenhausen distinguish the historically oriented idea of *Nachfolge* in the NT from the timeless *Nachahmung* in the second century, he also regards the Martyrdom of Polycarp as having advanced another step: Polycarp does not *consciously* imitate Christ; we see "marvellous dispensations from which it is deduced that Polycarp is to be imitated"; the martyr is an organ "through which Christ himself 'from heaven above' has revealed the evangelical norm of martyrdom" (von Campenhausen, *Idee*, 57-59, 83-87). In part it is also the "systematic" nature of the parallelism which impresses von Campenhausen and leads him finally to take up Müller's thesis (in a refined form).

Unfortunately, von Campenhausen is somewhat unclear as to when he thinks such a systematic parallelism possible (*SHA*, 1957, 9, n. 15; 14-15). Moreover, his distinctions seem somewhat forced: 1 Corinthians 11:1 and Philippians 3:17 suggest that although the imitation of one who imitates Christ is differently oriented here and in Paul, a variant of the theme is hardly outside the range of possibilities in the second century. Note too that the imitation theme in Acts 7 is free "of everything that aims at a conscious imitation" (Surkau p. 118); and although this probably has a somewhat different significance there, it makes it difficult to regard the treatment of the theme in the Martyrdom of Polycarp as late on this score. We are not surprised to learn that the martyrs of Gaul prayed for their persecutors "as did Stephen the perfect martyr" (Eusebius, *H.E.* 5.2.5); Polycarp is similarly evaluated in our text.

The evidence of Eusebius is also ambiguous. It has been argued that Eusebius was interested in narrative and that this accounts for the omission (Baden, *PB*, 25 [1912/13], 78-79). This view receives some support from Eusebius' treatment of Philo's *De Vita Contemplativa*. In *H.E.* 2.17.3-13 he paraphrases and quotes *Vita* 1-29 (the rest of his summary is of no interest to us since he announces his intention of being selective). The following elements in *Vita* 1-29 are not represented in Eusebius' treatment: the reference to the Essenes and the distinction between Essenes and Therapeutai in terms of Aristotle's practical and theoretical ways of life (1); the account of the forms of idolatry avoided by the Therapeutai (3-9) and praise of their pure theism (10-13); praise of their self-abnegation, which is superior to that known to the Greeks (14-17); an account of their pious dreams

2. For he waited to be delivered up as did also the Lord [cf. Matt. 26:36-46 par] that we too might become his imitators "not only looking to our own interests but also to those of our neighbor"

---

and the schedule of their prayers (26–27). Sometimes (e.g., *H.E.* 2.17.5) Eusebius gives no indication that he is passing over material; and he tends to omit what is of less immediate "historical" interest. That may well be the case here with 1:1b–2:1.

1:1. *Blessed:* Cf. Polyc. Phil. 3:2. *Seal:* Of the martyr's death in 4 Maccabees 7:15; Eusebius, *H.E.* 5.2.3; of the martyr's death which ends persecution in Eusebius, *M.P.* 11.13; 13.5 (cf. 4 Macc. 18:4). *Martyrdom:* Of the older literature note particularly J. Geffcken, *Hermes,* 45 (1910), 481-501, and K. Holl (II, 68-114). See now N. Brox, *Zeuge und Maertyrer* (Munich, 1961). The term *martyria* in 4 Maccabees 12:16(A) seems to be a Christian variant. Geffcken's theory of a Stoic origin of the term has been generally abandoned (though Stoic themes—mediated largely through 4 Maccabees—enrich the conception of the martyr). There is also general agreement that whereas in the NT a *martys* may die because he "witnesses," in the acts of the martyrs a man is a *martys* because he dies. It is perhaps safe to say that the first *clear* "martyrological" sense of the term occurs in the Martyrdom of Polycarp; but how it developed is obscure; a specifically biblical starting point need not be assumed (see on Polyc. Phil. 7:1). *Again:* Or "from above" (*anōthen*). The latter translation is adopted by von Campenhausen (*Idee,* 83) to underscore the "normative" character of the Martyrdom of Polycarp. *Show us . . . martyrdom in accord with the gospel:* Surkau p. 134, n. 137—rightly, I think—resists von Campenhausen's emphasis on the "normative" character of the Martyrdom of Polycarp. Martyr acts are intended for "edification," not "instruction." Surkau takes 2:1 as his starting point: martyrdom is *no accidental disaster.* Thus the "necessity" which hangs over Polycarp (5:2; 12:3; 14:2) is like that which hung over Jesus. The theme is intended to encourage Christians to stand firm against Satan's wiles (3:1; 17:1) in the knowledge that God's will is being done (cf. 7:1). It is within this framework that the imitation theme moves. Still, 1:2 and chapter 4 do show a "normative" concern: one is not to rush into martyrdom but wait to be handed over, as did Polycarp—and Jesus. I think this may be understood, however, as a subordinate aspect of the broader theme: let God's will be done. God's hand is not to be forced. He decides whom he will choose for the combat (20:1). The purpose of narrating the acts of the martyr is to prepare those who will be called on to suffer (cf. 18:3) and to glorify God who has made his choice from among his servants (20:1). The Martyrdom of Polycarp is "normative," then, only in the sense that the Christian's orientation is determined by the evangelic prototype. All narrower concerns are subordinate. In 19:1 the phrase "in accord

[Phil. 2:4]. For it is the mark of true and firm love not only to desire one's own salvation but also that of all the brethren.

II. The noble martyrs of Christ (2:1-4)

2 Blessed, then, and noble are all the martyrdoms that have taken place by the will of God; for we must devoutly ascribe to God power over all things. 2. For who would not admire their nobility and patience and love of their Master? They endured being shredded with whips until the fabric of their flesh could be seen down to the veins and arteries within so that even the by-

---

with the gospel *of Christ*" seems to point to this wider interpretation of the imitation theme. 1:2. *For he waited . . . all the brethren:* This passage is loosely constructed so that any pressing of the logical force of the connectives is difficult. The thought seems to be this: Polycarp's waiting is to be imitated by Christians, since that corresponds to the fundamental principle of brotherly love enunciated by Paul in Philippians 2:4; the martyr did not rush out to martyrdom with a view to his own soul's salvation but kept the needs of the brethren in mind. The author is probably thinking of the repercussions caused by behavior like that of Quintus (ch. 4). Once again, this is no mechanical application of the passion narrative. *As did also the Lord:* In a similar context already in Hegesippus (Eusebius, *H.E.* 4.22.4). *We too . . . his imitators:* Perhaps "we too" as well as Polycarp; if so, "his" means "the Lord's" (Lightfoot); but it is more likely that the reference is to the imitation of Polycarp (cf. 19:1) and that the word "also" reflects the point that Polycarp was not concerned about only himself. The fact, however, that Philippians 2:6 is quoted in the letter of the martyrs of Gaul (Eusebius, *H.E.* 5.2.2) in close connection with the theme of the imitation of Christ suggests that it is also presupposed here.

2:1-4. Eusebius (*H.E.* 4.15.4) makes no reference to "but they themselves displayed . . . angels" (vss. 2c-3). Von Campenhausen (*SHA*, 1957, 10-11) regards it as an interpolation. But he is aware that there is no trace of the imitation theme in it. And the oblique reference to death by fire in vs. 3 (or is it simply a form of torture?) hardly robs 5:2 and 11:2 of their dramatic significance. Again Eusebius has culled out the essential narrative element.

2:1. *Noble:* Cf. 2 Maccabees 6:28, 31; 7:5, 11, 21; 8:16; 13:14; 4 Maccabees 6:10; 8:3; 16:16; 17:24; 1 Clement 5:1, 6; Eusebius, *H.E.* 5.1.7, 17, 19, 36; Martyrdom of Carpus 35 (the term is often associated with Greek views of virtue and the Stoic metaphor of the athlete). 2:2. *Admire:* Cf. 4 Maccabees 17:16 ("Who would not admire the athletes of the divine law?"). *Felt pity:* Cf. 4 Maccabees 6:12. *None of them muttered or groaned:* Cf. Eusebius, *H.E.* 5.1.51 (4

standers felt pity and wept; but they themselves displayed such nobility that none of them muttered or groaned, showing us all that the most noble martyrs of Christ in that hour under torture were absent from the flesh, or rather, that the Lord was at hand and was conversing with them. 3. And with their minds fixed on the grace of Christ they despised the tortures of this world purchasing at the cost of one hour eternal life. To them even the fire of their inhuman torturers was cold; for they held before their eyes escape from the eternal fire which is never quenched, and with the eyes of their heart they gazed upon the good things

---

Macc. 11:19; Mart. Isa. 5:14). *Absent from the flesh:* Absent, pertaining to the life beyond: Plato *Apology* 40e–41a; *Phaedo* 61e, 67b (cf. Epictetus, *Discourses* 3.24.4, 60, 105). Experienced by martyrs before death: Martyrdom of Carpus 39–40; Eusebius, *H.E.* 5.1.19, 24 (cf. 4 Macc. 7:13); Martyrdom of Perpetua 20.3; Martyrdom of Irenaeus 4.4, 12; Eusebius, *M.P.* 11.12. Parallels: 4 Maccabees 6:5–6 ("tortured as in a dream," the flesh "shredded" with "whips"); Palestinian Talmud, Berakoth 9.7, 14b (Akiba "smiles" as he is martyred when it comes time to recite the Shema); Philo, *Probus* 107-108 (Stoic heroes make "their soul a fugitive from the body" and rise above pain; cf. D.L., 9.59); Euripides, *Bacchae* 757-763 (invulnerability as a result of divine possession; see also Iamblichus, *De Mysteriis* 3.4). Our passage may echo shamanistic conceptions (invulnerability as a result of absence from the body) which are not without analogies in the Mediterranean world and which may also be related to Plato's doctrine of the soul (cf. M. Eliade, *Shamanism* [New York, 1964]). *Conversing with them:* Cf. Eusebius, *H.E.* 5.1.51, 56; Martyrdom of Perpetua 4.1. Jewish anticipations of the theme: Martyrdom of Isaiah 5.7; 4 Maccabees 6:6 (cf. Acts 7:55); Genesis Rabba 65.22 (cf. Fischel, *JQR*, 37 [1946/47], 367-369). Holl (II, 68 ff.) artificially isolated this "visionary" element to link the "martyr" with apostleship (cf. 1 Cor. 15:15; Acts 7:55) and (Judaeo-Christian) prophecy (cf. Rev. 11:3). Pagan conceptions of the prophetic powers of those about to die offer some analogy: Homer, *Iliad* 16.843-854; 22.355-360 (cf. Sextus Empiricus, *Adversus Mathematicos* 3.20-22); Plato, *Crito* 44a-b; Cicero, *De Divinatione* 1.30.63-64. 2:3. *Purchasing... eternal life:* Cf. 2 Maccabees 7:36; 4 Maccabees 15:3 (cf. 9:8-9). Also reminiscent of the Rabbinic emphasis on eternal reward (or the certainty of it) in the case of martyrs (Surkau pp. 49-50, 68-69, 132). But in the Christian acts the motif is not rooted in a profound concern for loyalty to the Torah as it is in the Jewish texts. *Cold:* So also 4 Maccabees 11:26 (cf. 18:15); but the Martyrdom of Polycarp moves beyond the Stoic-Maccabean emphasis on the constancy of "reason." *Angels:* For the angelic nature of the dead see Enoch 104–

reserved for those who have endured, "which neither ear has heard nor eye has seen, nor have entered the heart of man" [1 Cor. 2:9 (cf. Isa. 64:4; 65:17; Ps-Philo, *Biblical Antinquities* 26:13)], but which were shown by the Lord to them who were no longer men but already angels. 4. Likewise also those condemned to the wild beasts endured frightful torment: they were laid on trumpet shells and afflicted with various other kinds of torture, so that, if possible, he (the afflicter) might turn them to denial through prolonged torment.

III. Germanicus (3:1-2)

3 For the devil devised many things against them. But thanks be to God; for he did not prevail against any of them. For the most noble Germanicus gave courage to their timidity through

---

106; 2 Baruch 51:10; Mark 12:25; Hermas, Visions 2.2.7; Similitudes 9.25.2; Tertullian, *De Resurrectione Carnis* 62; Clement, *Eclogae* 57; Origen, *Homily 9.11 on Leviticus*. But 4 Maccabees 9:22 already knows of a martyr "transformed, as it were, by the fire into incorruptibility." In Judaism pious men, prophets, and martyrs were often thought to resemble angels (Fischel, *JQR*, 37 [1946/47], 381-382; cf. Esther 5:2 LXX; Acts 6:15; *Didascalia Apostolorum* 19). Later Christian ascetics were also regarded as "angelic" (R. Reitzenstein, *Historia Monachorum* [Göttingen, 1916], 89). 2:4. (*The afflicter*): Supplied from the antecedent participle (Schwartz, *De Pionio*, 7). *Trumpet shells:* In Eusebius, "trumpet shells from the sea and certain sharp spits." This does not point to a basically different form of the text but to difficulty over the word *kērykes*—usually "heralds," rarely "trumpet shells" (LSJ, 949). MSS c p y read *xiphē* ("swords"), and it is possible that this was a gloss which Eusebius represents by *obeliskoi*—not only "spits" but "anything shaped like a spit," including the blade of a two-edged sword (LSJ, 1196). Cf. 4 Maccabees 11:19.

3:1-2. Eusebius' paraphrase of this event (*H.E.* 4.15.5-6) introduces a number of peculiar details which have been regarded by von Campenhausen as pointing to a different form of the text (*SHA*, 1957, 17). But they hardly seem impressive when we take into account Eusebius' method: we note, for example, that here his expression "with the help of divine grace (*charis*)" is an editorial transformation of "thanks (*charis*) be to God"; that in *H.E.* 2.17.3 he shortens Philo's text, yet adds phrases like "and the women in their company" and "of those who came to them"; and that in the case of other documents he alters at times the sense of the original (Lawlor-Oulton, II, 20).

the endurance he showed. He also fought gloriously with wild beasts. For when the proconsul wished to persuade him and told him to have compassion on his youth, he forcibly pulled the wild beast to (himself) of his own accord desirous of taking leave as quickly as possible of their unjust and lawless way of life. 2. Consequently the whole multitude, amazed at the nobility of the godly and pious race of Christians, began shouting: "Away with the atheists! Let Polycarp be sought!"

IV. Quintus (4:1)

4 Now one named Quintus, a Phrygian, recently arrived from

3:1. *The devil:* Cf. Eusebius, H.E. 5.1.27; Martyrdom of Carpus 17; Martyrdom of Perpetua 10.7. *For he did not prevail,* etc.: More naturally, "for he did not prevail against them all." Schwartz (*De Pionio,* 7-8) goes on to trace a complex evolution of the text which he thinks arose from embarrassment at the remark. Our translation, however, rests on a looseness of expression well attested in the Hellenistic period (L. Radermacher, *Neutestamentliche Grammatik* [Tübingen, 1925], 219-220). (Lightfoot's objection that the statement is not true in light of chapter 4 presses the text too closely; cf. Acts 4:32; 5:1 ff. By "them" in verse 1 is meant those praised in 2:4 or 2:1-4.) *Thanks be to God:* Cf. 1 Corinthians 15:57, etc. This is hardly a sigh of relief that at least some remained firm. Germanicus is not regarded as an exception in so far as he was martyred but in so far as he encouraged all the others. There is no sign of mass persecution in Smyrna. The Martyrdom of Polycarp speaks only of the twelve Philadelphian martyrs (including Germanicus; see on 19:1), Quintus (along with a few others), and Polycarp; and since the latter brought the "persecution" to an end, no others were involved in it. The martyrs were a select few (cf. 20:1). *Compassion on his youth:* Cf. 4 Maccabees 8:10. *Forcibly: prosbiasamenos* (cf. Ign. Rom. 5:2) as distinguished from *parabiasamenos,* which characterizes the activity of Quintus (ch. 4). *Taking leave:* Cf. Martyrdom of Carpus 39–40 (Plato, Apol. 40e–41a). **3:2.** *Atheists:* A charge brought by pagans against Jews and extended to include also Christians (Dio 67.14). The charge is countered by Justin (*Apol.* 1.5.3; 6.1; 13.1; 46.3) and Athenagoras (*Leg.* 3 ff.). That Christians and Epicureans are linked as "atheists" by Alexander (Lucian, *Alexander* 25, 38) is regarded by Caster (*Lucien* [Paris, 1937], 349), as a vicious form of anti-Epicurean slander. See further on 9:2. *Sought:* Contrary to the rescript of Trajan (Pliny, *Ep.* 10.97.1).

4:1. The position of chapter 4 dissociates Quintus' failure from all that has been said in 2:1–3:2 and underscores the contrast between

Phrygia, became frightened when he saw the wild beasts. It was he who had pressured both himself and some others to come forward voluntarily. Him the proconsul earnestly entreated and persuaded to take the oath and to sacrifice. So then, brethren, we do not praise those coming forward of their own accord, for that is not the teaching of the gospel.

V. Polycarp's withdrawal (5:1-2)

5 Now the most marvelous Polycarp was not disturbed when he first heard the news but wanted to stay in the city. The others,

---

him and Polycarp. The scheme is artificial; chapter 4 may even be an interpolation (for the connection between ch. 3 and ch. 5 is disturbed by it). If so, it is a pre-Eusebianic interpolation (Eusebius, *H.E.* 4.15.7-8). But I think the report falls into these artificially arranged panels to distinguish clearly between a proper and improper approach to martyrdom (cf. 3:1). If the interruption still seems too marked, the reason may be that chapter 4 was added in Smyrna during the final stages of the letter's composition (Simonetti, *GIF*, 9 [1956], 339-340).

Von Campenhausen, who believes chapter 4 to be an interpolation, assumes that the imitation theme here ("the teaching of the gospel" —missing in Eusebius) was added even later (with 1:1b-2:1); the redactor was lucky enough to have provided for him an account which illustrated his point so well (*SHA*, 1957, 12, 18-20)! Eusebius' omission of the imitation theme, however, is hardly significant in view of his total rewriting of the passage.

Many regard the term "Phrygian" as pointing to Montanism, which was "the heresy according to the Phrygians" (Eusebius, *H.E.* 5.16.1) and which was enthusiastic about martyrdom (Tertullian, *De Fuga* 9; *De Anima* 55). According to Eusebius, Montanism arose in A.D. 172 (cf. Meinhold, PWK, XXI, 1678-1679). Chapter 4, then, was inserted after the composition of the letter (*ca.* 155?), or the whole letter is to be dated later (Keim, pp. 119-122), or the date of Polycarp's martyrdom must be set later (Grégoire, *AB*, 69 [1951], 1-38). The last thesis runs up against formidable objections (Telfer, *JTS*, 3 [1952], 79-83; Marrou, *AB*, 71 [1953], 5-20). The second view rests on the identification of anachronisms throughout the text which, with doubtful exceptions, are unimpressive. As to the first theory, it may be noted that not every Phrygian was a Montanist (cf. Eusebius, *H.E.* 5.1.49). And there are still those who have not been convinced by Labriolle that Epiphanius' date for the rise of Montanism—A.D. 156/157—is wrong (Simonetti, *GIF*, 9 [1956], 332-338; Lawlor-Oulton, II, 180-181).

5:1-2. Müller's reasons (*Ueberlieferungsgeschichte*, 36-41) for eliminating most of chapter 5 are inadequate (for the Armenian text

however, tried to persuade him to withdraw; and he did withdraw to a farm not far away from the city and stayed there with a few friends doing nothing night and day but praying for all men and for the churches throughout the world, as was his custom. 2. And while in prayer he had a vision three days before he was arrested; and he saw his pillow burning up with fire; and he turned and said to those with him: "I must be burned alive."

VI. Polycarp's arrest (6:1–7:3)

6 And when his pursuers persisted, he moved to another farm, and immediately his pursuers were upon the scene; and when they did not find him, they apprehended two young slaves, one of whom confessed when tortured. [2. For it was quite impossible for him to remain hidden since in fact his betrayers were members of his household. And the police captain who fittingly bore the same name—Herod, as he was called—was anxious to bring him into the stadium; thus he was to fulfill his own destiny by becoming a partner with Christ, and his betrayers were to suffer

---

of Eusebius is no sure guide; the imitation theme here is tenuous [cf. Matt. 26:36 ff.; Luke 22:39 ff.; John 18:1]; and it is hard to read chapter 15 without being convinced that Polycarp was in some significant sense "burned alive"). Müller's complex reconstruction of the original text is not convincing. Schwartz (*De Pionio*, 9), however, has persuaded some that Eusebius, *H.E.* 4.15.9 (Polycarp had a vision "by night" and then "awoke") is closer to the original than the present chapter. Eusebius, in my opinion, is simply making another effort to provide a psychologically more satisfying account; the contradiction, then, with 12:3 (*i.e.*, *H.E.* 4.15.28) is of the historian's own making. 5:2. *Vision:* Foreknowledge of one's death plays an important role in other Christian martyrdoms (Mart. Perp. 4.1-6, etc.), in the biography of the Hellenistic "divine man" (Philostratus, *Vit. Apollon.* 7.38), in Jewish martyrdoms (Mart. Isa. 1.7; cf. Fischel, *JQR*, 37 [1946/47], 369), in the Gospels (Mark 8:31, etc.). For the perspective from which this element is viewed in the Martyrdom of Polycarp see p. 53.

6:1–7:3. The section 6:2–7:1a seems to be an interpolation. Eusebius (*H.E.* 4.15.11-14) omits it, and it contains historical notes that we would ordinarily expect to be of interest to him (see p. 52). Two MSS (c v) omit part of the passage. The clumsiness of the language in 6:2—with or without the emendations of Zahn and Schwartz (*De Pionio*, 9-10)—is noteworthy. The imitation theme emerges here in a crass form (cf. Matt. 26:47-56; Mark 7:24; 15:42; John 13:18; 18:3) and seems in part to be unmotivated within the framework of

the punishment of Judas himself. 7 Taking the slave, then, mounted policemen and horsemen armed in their usual way set out on Friday about supper hour "coming forth as against a robber" (Matt. 26:55).] And converging on him late in the evening they found him lying down in a little room upstairs; now even from there he could have gone elsewhere; but he decided not to, saying: "God's will be done" [Matt. 26:42, 53; Acts 21:14 (cf. Matt. 6:10)]. 2. So when he heard that they had arrived, he went down and conversed with them while those who saw him marveled at his age and composure and were surprised that the eagerness to apprehend an old man like him was so great. Then he immediately ordered as much food and drink to be set before them at that time as they wished; and he asked them to give him an hour to pray undisturbed. 3. They gave him permission; and he stood and prayed so filled with the grace of God that for two hours he could not stop speaking; and those who heard him were amazed, and many regretted that they had come after so godly an old man.

---

the narrative as a whole (the announcement of the punishment of Polycarp's "betrayers" hangs in the air). Apart from this interpolation, it is artificial to find the imitation theme in the flight to the farm (John 18.1), in Polycarp's long prayer (John 17), in the supper set for his enemies (Matt. 26:20, 26-29).

6:1. *Upon the scene:* It is unclear whether this refers to the first farm (Kleist, *ACW*, VI, 200) or the second (Eusebius). The former seems more likely. The "little room upstairs," (7:1), then, was located on the second farm. 6:2. *Police captain:* Cf. 8:2. In Smyrna almost certainly one of the "generals" and "selected by the governor of the province from a list of ten persons drawn up by the Council" (Cadoux p. 199). 7:1. *Friday:* The Jewish term "Preparation" is used. Probably an imitation of John 19:14, 31, 42; Mark 15:42 (but see also Did. 8:1). *Mounted policemen: diōgmitai,* a technical term for constables in Asia Minor (*CIG* [Boechk], 3831). 7:2. *Surprised that:* For this use of *thaumazein ei* (where the cause of surprise is spoken of somewhat delicately) see Xenophon, *Historia Graeca* 2.3.53. *At that time:* Possibly "late as it was" (Kleist, *ACW*, VI, 93). If so, however, there is no break in the course of events from 7:1b on to the end of the martyrdom of Polycarp. Yet at 7:1b it is "late in the evening," whereas the martyrdom took place during the day. Is it possible that we are asked to imagine the constables closing in at night (7:1b) and appearing before the doors of the house the next morning (7:2)? Is that why Polycarp may yet have escaped? If so, "at that time" refers

VII. On the way (8:1-3)

8 Now when he had at last ended his prayer, in which he recalled all those whom he had ever met both small and great, high and low, and all the catholic church throughout the world, the hour came for departure, and they set him on an ass and brought

---

to the early morning. 7:3. *Grace:* In the "Hellenistic" sense of an infused power manifesting itself in extraordinary religious phenomena (Torrance pp. 98-99; cf. Eusebius, *H.E.* 8.12.11; *M.P.* 9.3; 4.8; 11.19). For the content of the prayer see Polycarp to the Philippians 12:3.
8:1. *Hour . . . ass . . . [Great Sabbath]*: Cf. John 17:1; 12:14; 19:31. The Great Sabbath indicated in medieval Jewry, the Sabbath before Passover and in the early Church (but not before the age of Chrysostom) the Saturday before Easter (Schwartz, *Ostertafeln,* 127). In the latter sense it would be out of place in a Quartodeciman community like Smyrna (Eusebius, *H.E.* 5.24.16). This is a key point in Keim's (pp. 103-106) late dating of the Martyrdom of Polycarp. It is more likely that the phrase is an imitation of John 19:31; if so, it may represent an interpolation reflecting the same impulse that led to dating the arrest on "the Preparation" (7:1). See also chapter 21. In any event, the "hour" and the "ass" offer only very tenuous parallels to the Gospels (the situation hardly demands that Polycarp remount the ass in verse 3 if it were mentioned in the original text of verse 1). The initial silence of Polycarp in verse 2 offers a somewhat more convincing parallel (Mark 14:61); but even this motif occurs elsewhere (Maximus of Tyre, 3.7e [ed. Hobein]). 8:2. *Nicetes:* Cf. 17:2. The name is used of a Smyrnaean in *CIG* (Boeckh), 3359, and was borne by a famous Sophist who took up residence in the city in the time of Vespasian (Cadoux pp. 247-248). *Carriage:* Eusebius (*H.E.* 4.15.15) uses Greek *ochēma* instead of the Latin (Celtic) *carucca.* But the refinement seems to have been made before his time (Schwartz, *De Pionio,* 10-11). *'Caesar is Lord':* The title Lord was first allowed by Gaius. The Greek form occurs on Greek coins in the reign of Antoninus Pius (A.D. 138–161). According to Mommsen (*Staatsrecht,* II, 735-740), the title was fundamentally political, not religious, in nature. But Domitian (Suetonius, *Domitian* 13) had already spoken of himself (unofficially) as *dominus et deus noster;* and the Christian tended to understand the term against the background of his own confession, "Jesus is Lord" (1 Cor. 12:3; Rom. 10:9; cf. Tertullian, *Apology* 34). There were high feelings of imperial loyalty throughout Asia Minor (Cadoux pp. 229-240). *Sacrificing:* So BAG, 293, and Lampe p. 525; the verb may also mean "offer incense" (Lightfoot; LSJ, 635). What the author has in mind is illustrated by Pliny, *Ep.* 10.96.5, where we learn that those denying they are Chris-

him into the city. [It was a Great Sabbath.] 2. And the police captain, Herod, and his father, Nicetes, met him; they transferred him to their carriage and sitting down beside him tried to persuade him, saying: "Why, what is wrong with saying, 'Caesar is Lord,' and sacrificing, and so forth, and thus being saved?" At first he did not answer them, but when they persisted, he said: "I am not going to do what you advise me." 3. Since they had failed

---

tians must "supplicate with incense and wine" the image of the emperor brought in along with images of the gods (cf. Tertullian, *Apology* 30). Prayer and sacrifice (annually) on behalf of the emperor played an important role in civic rites from the early days of the empire (Dio 44.6; 58.3; 75.14; Mommsen, *Staatsrecht*, II, 784-785). The legal significance of the demand to sacrifice is obscure. Perhaps the soundest view is this: The sacrifice does not really signify a falling away from Christianity but adherence to the state religion; Christianity, then, was not persecuted "as such," but Christians were regarded as guilty of *maiestas* for unwillingness to adhere to paganism; in the Martyrdom of Polycarp, however, we begin to see popular animosity against Christianity "as such" (Tacitus, *Ann.* 15.44.5) hardening into an official attitude (Sild pp. 61-88). **8:3.** *Briskly:* The MSS read *prothymōs meta spoudēs;* but the latter phrase seems to a dittography from the first sentence of the verse (Schwartz, *De Pionio*, 11). *As he was led,* etc.: This is a reconstruction involving the first lines of chapter 9. The MSS read: "He walked along briskly and vigorously, being led into the stadium with the uproar in the stadium so great that no one could be heard," etc. Eusebius (*H.E.* 4.15.16-17) reads: "But without turning around, as though he had suffered no injury, he walked along briskly and vigorously being led into the stadium. Now (*de*) with the uproar in the stadium so great that it could not be heard by many (Mart. Polyc.: that no one could be heard), a voice came from heaven to Polycarp as he was entering, 'Be strong, Polycarp, and play the man.' And no one saw the speaker, but many of ours (Mart. Polyc.: those of ours who were present) heard the voice; (Mart. Polyc.: then, *loipon*) as he was brought forward, therefore, great was the uproar of those who heard that Polycarp had been arrested. Then (*loipon*) the proconsul asked him as he was brought forward. . . ." Schwartz's solution (*De Pionio*, 11-13) seems best: The MSS of the Martyrdom of Polycarp correctly separate 8:3 from 9:1. But Eusebius' readings "heard by many" and "many of ours" are best. "Those of ours who were present" (Mart. Polyc.) represents an effort to soften the contradiction: "not heard by many"/"many of ours heard." But what is it that "could not be heard"? The obscurity was corrected by reading "that no one could be heard" (Mart. Polyc.), although this introduced a fresh contradiction ("no one could be heard"/"many of ours heard"). Someone tried putting the noise *after*

to persuade him, they uttered threats and hurriedly pulled him off so that as he was descending from the carriage he scraped his shin. And without turning around, he walked along briskly as though he had suffered no injury. As he was led into the stadium with the uproar so great that it was not heard by many. . . .

VIII. Polycarp's trial (9:1–11:2)

9 [Now a voice from heaven came to Polycarp as he was entering the stadium: "Be strong, Polycarp, and play the man!" (Josh. 1:6, 7, 9.) No one saw the speaker, but many of ours heard the

---

the miracle; hence the doublet. The confusion concerning the position of *loipon* seems to reflect a similar effort to allow the voice to be heard despite the noise (Reuning pp. 27-30). Behind the confusion, according to Schwartz, lies the interpolation of the remarks concerning the miraculous voice. The restored text reads: "Now when he was led into the stadium and the noise was so great that not many heard that he had been apprehended, the proconsul asked him . . ." (This eliminates the doublets and makes clear what "could not be heard by many.") The proclamation of the herald in 12:1 is to be taken as the first indication that the crowd as a whole learned of Polycarp's presence.

9:1–11:2. If Schwartz's view of the text of 8:3–9:2a is right (see above), the trial takes place in a somewhat less hectic atmosphere than that suggested by the interpolation. The noise in the stadium attended the wild-beast hunts that were all but concluded (12:2). Only a few hear of Polycarp's arrival (8:3–9:1 reconstructed); he is examined by the proconsul (9:2–11:2); the result of that inquiry is made public by means of a herald (12:1). Friends of Polycarp may have attended him (cf. 5:1; 17:2; 18:1) and heard what was said.

The trial takes the form of a *cognitio*—an administrative action which simplified judicial procedures (Pliny, *Ep.* 10.96.1; cf. Mommsen, *Strafrecht*, 35-54; Sherwin-White pp. 1-23). That the mob could play some role in such a trial is known to us from the Gospels and from a late Anatolian inscription discussed by Grégoire (*Persécutions*, 28).

The Martyrdom of Polycarp as a whole conforms to the literary type emerging already in the accounts of the Maccabean martyrs; but in chapters 9–11 we hear an echo of the protocol style characteristic of another branch of martyr acts. The skeptical Geffcken (using especially Eusebius, *H.E.* 5.1.20 as a standard) finds only in the question as to Polycarp's identity (9:2) a "shadow" of the legal process (*Hermes*, 45 [1910], 488-490). Such questions, however, were only a beginning, and we shall see that skepticism about all the elements in chapters 9–11 is unwarranted.

9:1. *Stadium:* Or "arena." In Smyrna it measured 200 by 40 yards in all and was located close to the southern wall of the city (Cadoux

voice. And then as he was brought forward, there was a great uproar now that they heard] that Polycarp had been apprehended. 2. [So when he was brought forward] the proconsul asked him whether he was Polycarp; and when he admitted it, he tried to persuade him to deny, saying: "Respect your age" and all the other things they usually say: "Swear by the Genius of Caesar, change your mind, say, 'Away with the atheists.'" Polycarp

---

p. 178). *A voice from heaven:* Reminiscent of the *bath qol* which played an important role in accounts of Jewish martyrdoms (e.g., *Abodah Zarah* 18a). Here it may represent another application of the imitation theme (John 12:28). 9:2. *Proconsul:* The supreme judicial authority was the Roman governor. He may have been in Smyrna to attend the league festival of the province of Asia held yearly in honor of the emperor. Smyrna was one of the four sites in which it was celebrated (Cadoux pp. 230-231, 355-356). *"Respect your age":* Cf. 4 Maccabees 5:7, 12. For the offer of amnesty see Passion of the Martyrs of Scilli 1 ("You can gain the indulgence of our lord the emperor if you regain your senses"). *Genius* (or "Fortune") *of Caesar:* Cf. Passion of the Martyrs of Scilli 1-5; Martyrdom of Apollonius 3. For the theological underpinnings of the refusal see Tertullian, *Apology* 32; Origen, *Exhortation to Martyrdom* 7. The oath goes back to Hellenistic times (Tarn-Griffith, *Hellenistic Civilization* [London, 1952], 340) and was introduced in Rome by Julius Caesar (Dio 44.6; cf. 57.8; 58.2; 59.3, 9; *CIL*, II, 172; Suetonius, *Caligula* 27). In our period Greek "Fortune" and Roman "Genius" function alike; according to Origen (*Contra Celsum* 8.65), some say that "'Fortune' is only a mode of expression like an opinion or disagreement," whereas others say that "people who swear by the Genius of the Roman emperor are swearing by his daemon." On one interpretation, the demand to swear such an oath was an arbitrary device selected to show up Christians at a time when Christianity as such was the crime (Weiss pp. 810-817). It is more likely, however, that the oath was bound up with the charge of *maiestas;* the veneration of the emperor's Genius made the old principle *deorum iniuriae dis curae* (Tacitus, Ann. 1.73.5) obsolete (Mommsen, *Staatsrecht*, II, 783-784; Sild pp. 93, 104-106). *Atheists:* Cf. 3:2. There is no trace in legal literature that "atheism" was regarded as a crime (Mommsen, *HZ*, 64 [1890], 393-394). On one interpretation, then, the action against Christians was solely an administrative matter; Christianity as such was outlawed not on the basis of express law or formal edict but because Christians "were held to be unsuitable or subversive or demoralizing" (A. D. Nock, *HTR*, 45 [1952], 217; cf. Ramsay pp. 196-223). It is more likely, however, that Christian "atheists" were open to the more serious charge of *maiestas*, since they could point to no province of the empire in which their way of life was traditional; possibly by the time

looked sternly at the whole crowd of lawless heathen in the stadium, indicating them with a wave of the hand, groaned and looked up to heaven, and said: "Away with the atheists!" 3. When the proconsul persevered and said: "Take the oath and I will let you go; revile Christ," Polycarp replied: "I have served him eighty-six years and in no way has he dealt unjustly with me; so how can I blaspheme my king who saved me?"

10 Since he persisted and said: "Swear by Caesar's Genius," he answered: "If you vainly expect that I will swear by Caesar's Genius, as you suggest, and pretend to be ignorant who I am, listen (to what I say) openly: I am a Christian. If you want to

---

of the Martyrdom of Polycarp identification as a Christian was all but regarded as proof of treason (Mommsen, *Strafrecht*, 573-575; Sild pp. 61, 79). *Looked . . . at the . . . crowd . . . and said:* Cf. Polycarp to the Philippians 7:1.

9:3. *Revile Christ:* Cf. Pliny, *Ep.* 10.96.5-6. Possibly an indication that Christianity as such was persecuted; but the significance of action against Christians on the basis of the "very name" (Pliny, *Ep.* 10.96.2) is ambiguous (Sild pp. 51-58). *Eighty-six years:* Some scholars date this from Polycarp's baptism (cf. the language used by Jerome, *De Vita Hilarii* 45) and assume that he was considerably older (Zahn, *Ignatius*, 326-327). Others invert the argument: Since it is difficult for a number of reasons to imagine that Polycarp was older than eighty-six (e.g., he undertook a strenuous journey to Rome at the time of Anicetus, who was bishop in A.D. 155-166 at the earliest), and since Polycarp could speak of himself this way only as a baptized Christian, he must have been baptized as an infant (J. Jeremias, *Infant Baptism in the First Four Centuries* [Philadelphia, 1960], 59-63). Both interpretations press the language too narrowly. It means, as Nautin p. 72, n. 1 suggests: "I have always served Christ and I am not going to cease doing so at the age of eighty-six" (cf. Eusebius, *H.E.* 5.24.7). Consequently it is impossible to deduce anything from this statement about the likelihood of infant baptism in the case of Polycarp (cf. K. Aland, *Did the Early Church Baptize Infants?* [Philadelphia, 1963], 70-74). *King:* The contrast between Christ the King and the Roman emperor ("king"; cf. Polyc. Phil. 12:3) is fully expressed in the Passion of the Martyrs of Scilli 6.

10:1. *Vainly expect:* The translation "vainly imagine" is too weak in view of the *hina* clause (Schwartz, *De Pionio*, 13; cf. L. Radermacher, *Neutestamentliche Grammatik* [Tübingen, 1925], 191-193). *Openly:* The *parrēsia* of the martyr is to be understood from the ancient ideal of "boldness" before civil authorities (E. Peterson, in

learn the teaching of Christianity, name the day and hear (about it)." 2. The proconsul said: "Persuade the People." Polycarp replied: "To you indeed I have considered myself accountable; for we have been taught to render fit honor to rulers and authorities appointed by God in so far as it is not injurious to us; as for these, I do not consider myself bound to make my defense before them."

11 The proconsul said: "I have wild beasts; I will throw you to them unless you change your mind." He replied: "Call for them; for a change from better to worse is impossible for us; but it is laudable to change from evil to good." 2. He said to him again: "I will have you consumed with fire, if you despise wild beasts, unless you change your mind." Polycarp replied: "You threaten fire which burns for an hour and is soon quenched; for you are ignorant of the fire of the coming judgment and eternal punishment reserved for the wicked. But why do you wait? Come, do what you will!"

Reinhold-Seeberg-Festschrift [Leipzig, 1929], 293, n. 2). It is also characteristic of the acts of the pagan martyrs and the Stoic-Cynic heroes (Musurillo pp. 239-240, 225). Polycarp steps before us "as the heroic warrior" (Campenhausen, *Idee*, 152-153). Yet Polycarp's boldness has to do only with his confession of being a Christian and does not characterize his responses as a whole (language contemptuous of the authorities is characteristic of the *later* Christian acts; Delehaye, *Genres*, 158-159). Cf. 11:2. In any event, an important inscription has removed doubts concerning the possibility of such "boldness" (Roussel-de Visscher, *Syria*, 22/23 [1941/43], 173-200). *I am a Christian:* Cf. Martyrdom of Carpus 5; Martyrdom of Justin 3.4; Eusebius, *H.E.* 5.1.20; Passion of the Martyrs of Scilli 9-13, Martyrdom of Apollonius 2 (cf. 2 Macc. 6:6). The question which the statement presupposes was of decisive importance for Pliny (*Ep.* 10.96.3). Again the exact legal significance it had is debatable (see above). **10:2.** *The People:* The proconsul uses the term *dēmos*—the People in their official capacity (Cadoux p. 187). This may have represented an (unsuccessful) attempt to shift responsibility for the martyrdom. *We have been taught:* Cf. Polycarp to the Philippians 12:3.

11:1. *Change:* Greek *metanoia*, which in the Bible means "repentance." This may represent a play on words. But especially in view of the Platonic ring of the sentence as a whole—for the change from "better" to "worse" see Plato, *Republic* 381b-c; Philo, *Leges Allegoriae* 1.72; 3.246; *De Specialibus Legibus* 1.62; 4.86; *De Aeternitate Mundi*

IX. The martyrdom of Polycarp: Preliminaries (12:1–13:3)

12 As he spoke these and many other things he became filled with courage and joy, and his face was suffused with grace so that not only did he not collapse in terror at what was said, but on the contrary the proconsul was amazed; and he sent his herald into the middle of the stadium to announce three times: "Polycarp has confessed that he is a Christian." 2. When this had been said by the herald, the whole crowd of Gentiles and Jews who lived in Smyrna cried out with uncontrolled anger and with a loud shout: "This is the teacher of Asia, the father of the Christians, the destroyer of our gods, the one who teaches many not

---

42–43—I doubt that the author is conscious of any specifically biblical sense of the term. 11:2. *Fire:* Cf. 2:3. In Roman law being burned alive was considered worthy of *summi supplicii appellatio* (*Dig.* 48.19.28) and was reserved especially for enemies, traitors, and *humiles personae* in general (48.19.8; 48.19.28.11). *The coming judgment:* The pronouncement of the just retribution (cf. 2 Macc. 7:19; 4 Macc. 9:32; 10:10-11; Mart. Isa. 5.9), along with Polycarp's despisal of the fire which burns but an hour, lends to his "boldness" less of the heroic, cooly apologetic, or abusive tone of the Hellenistic martyrs and more of that peculiar blend of prophetic, ascetical, and dogmatic qualities that characterizes the early Greek fathers. (It must be confessed that 11:1-2 as a whole, with its careful antitheses, appears to reflect considerable reworking of whatever may have passed between Polycarp and the proconsul; moreover, the motivation for the fiery death of Polycarp is explained differently in 12:2-3).

12:1. *Grace:* Cf. 7:3. For the facial transformation see 1 Enoch 38:4; 2 Baruch 51:3; Acts 6:15 (Matt. 17:2; Luke 9:29); more natural is the beauty of the Jewish martyr in 2 Maccabees 6:18; for the link between grace and extraordinary physical appearance in Hellenistic sources see H. D. Betz, *Lukian von Samosata* (Berlin, 1961), 132-133. Cf. Eusebius, *H.E.* 5.1.35; Martyrdom of Marianus and James 9.2; the theme is closely related to 2:3. *Three times:* Cf. Pliny, *Ep.* 10.96.3. By placing a full stop before *tris*, we get the herald announcing (once) that Polycarp has confessed three times. This would agree even more closely with the remarks of Pliny. 12:2. *Jews:* There had long been a sizable community of Jews in Smyrna (Cadoux pp. 303-404). Jews, however, could hardly have said the things that follow. The imitation theme may have something to do with their presence here (Simon pp. 150-151). *Asia:* This is the reading of m and Eusebius. "Impiety" is read by the other Greek MSS and is accepted by Hilgenfeld as fitting the setting (cf. Cadoux p. 361, n. 3). But we are probably dealing with a Christian estimation projected on

to sacrifice nor to worship." Saying this, they began to shout and ask for the Asiarch, Philip, to set a lion upon Polycarp. But he said that he had no authority to do so since he had ended the wild-beast hunts. 3. Then it occurred to them to begin shouting all together that he burn Polycarp alive. For it was necessary that the vision be fulfilled [cf. John 18:32] which had appeared to him in connection with his pillow when he saw it burning as he prayed and he turned and said prophetically to those of the faithful who were with him: "I must be burned alive" [cf. 5:2].

13 This, then, took place with such great speed—more quickly than can be related: the crowd wasted no time gathering wood and fuel from the shops and baths; the Jews were especially energetic, as they usually are, in lending a hand in this. 2. When the pyre was prepared, he readily took off all his garments and loosened his belt; he also made an effort to take off his shoes though he had not been used to doing this since each of the faithful always hurried that he might be the first to touch his skin; for he was adorned with every (power) because of his goodly

---

the crowd (though for the possibility that Polycarp enjoyed a high reputation among pagans see the curious remark in Eusebius, *H.E.* 5.20.4); moreover, "impiety" probably arose from the later tendency to generalize the acts of the martyrs (Müller, *RQ*, 22 [1908], 5). *Asiarch:* This official presided over the league festival (Cadoux pp. 231, 355-356). A Gaius Julius Philippus is known from inscriptions and seems to have been Asiarch under Antoninus Pius (inscriptions dated between 149 and, it seems, 153) and procurator under Marcus Aurelius (Lightfoot, I, 628-635, 666-667; III, 383-385). If this is our Philip, a date for Polycarp's martyrdom sometime in the sixth decade of the second century is supported (cf. Harrison pp. 277-283). Lightfoot has shown that Asiarchs probably held office for four years (III, 413) and that some held the office twice or even three times (III, 414). See Martydom of Polycarp 21. *Wild-beast hunts:* For the games in Smyrna see Martyrdom of Pionius 18:8 (Cadoux p. 297).

13:1. *Such great speed—more quickly than:* Possibly a conflated reading (Schwartz, *De Pionio*, 14). *Baths:* For the numerous baths in Smyrna see Cadoux p. 181. 13:2. *Touch his skin:* Cf. Mark 5:25-34; Acts 5:15; 19:11, 12. The bishop takes on the dimensions of a "divine man"; but there is as yet no talk of miracles. See 17:1. *Before his martyrdom:* Eusebius' reading—"before his old age" (*H.E.* 4.15.30) —is possibly correct (Schwartz, *De Pionio*, 14; Delehaye, *AB*, 38 [1920], 201, regards both readings as variant efforts to deal with a

way of life even before his martyrdom. 3. Without delay the material prepared for the pyre was set about him. And as they were also about to nail him, he said: "Let me be as I am; for he who makes it possible for me to endure the fire will also make it possible for me to remain on the pyre unmoved without the security of nails."

X. The martyrdom of Polycarp: The prayer (14:1-3)

14 They did not nail him, but set about binding him. Now when he had put his hands behind him and had been bound, like a splendid ram from a great flock (ready) for sacrifice, prepared as a burnt offering acceptable unto God, he looked up to heaven and said:

"*Lord God Almighty*,[1]
Father [2] of your *beloved* [3] and *blessed* [4] *Son* [3,4,5] *Jesus Christ* [2] *through whom* [6] we have received *knowledge* [7] of you,

[1] Amos 3:13; 4:13; 5:8, 14-16; 9:15; Hos. 12:5; Rev. 4:8; 11:17; 15:3; 16:7; 21:22. ApCo 8.15.2 (Eucharistic; cf. Did. 10:3).
[2] ApCo 8.15.2, "Master, God Almighty, Father of your Christ, your blessed Son" (Eucharistic).
[3] Matt. 12:8, *pais* . . . *agapētos* (the latter not in Isa. 42:1, which is quoted here); cf. Mark 1:1; 9:7; Diog. 8.11. 1 Clem. 59:2, *ēgapēmenou paidos* ("liturgical").
[4] ApCo 8.15.2 (Eucharistic; cf. Matt. 12:8).
[5] Isa. 52:13 (*pais*: God's "servant"); Acts 3:13, 26; 4:27, 30; Barn. 9:2; Diog. 8.9, 11; 9.1. 1 Clem. 59:2-4 ("liturgical"). ApCo 8.15.2 (Eucharistic; cf. Did. 9:2-3; 10:2). For *pais* as "son" see Mart. Just. 2.4, 5; ApCo 8.40.1; the use of the term in Mart. Polyc. 20:2 suggests that this is its meaning here.
[6] This formula regularly has to do with Christ (1 Clem. 58:2; 59:2, 3; 61:3; ch. 64; ch. 65; 2 Clem. 20:5).
[7] 1 Clem. 59.2 ("liturgical"). Cf. Did. 9:2-3; 10:2 (Eucharistic?); ApCo 8.11.2 (liturgical).

---

dittography of *politeias*). *Adorned:* Some translate "honored." But the verb does not ever seem to mean that. The textual confusion shows that some difficulty was felt. Apparently the sentence was regarded as an explanation of the enthusiasm of the faithful to serve Polycarp. But to us it looks more like an explanation of their desire to touch his flesh. Schwartz (*De Pionio*, 14-15) assumes that originally the text read "with every charism," or something of that kind.

14:1-3. It is unlikely that this chapter reflects the imitation theme (cf. John 17). Polycarp may well have uttered a prayer at this point (cf. Mart. Carp. 41; Mart. Pion. 21.7-9; 4 Macc. 6:27-29). Neverthe-

God of angels [8] and *powers* [9]
and *every created thing* [10]
and all *the race of the just* [11]
who dwell before you,

2. *I bless you* [12]
because *you have considered me worthy* [13] of this day and hour [14]
to receive *a portion,* [15] among *the number* [16] of the martyrs,
in the *cup* [17] of *your Christ* [18]
unto *the resurrection of eternal life* [19]
both of soul and body [20]
in the *incorruption* [21] of the Holy Spirit,

---

[8] "God of angels" not in LXX or early Christian literature (Reuning p. 35); but see ApCo 8.12:8; *Anaph. Serap.* 13.8-10.

[9] 1 Kings 17:1; Ps. 59:5 (cf. Judith 9:14; 13:4). Cf. *Anaph. Serap.* 13.11 ("Lord of powers").

[10] Judith 9:12 (cf. Col. 1:15).

[11] Hermas, Sim. 9.17.5 (of Christians); cf. Mart. Polyc. 17:1.

[12] Acts of Paul and Thecla 24 (a prayer). Cf. Josephus, *Ant.* 7.380; Luke 1:64; 2:28; 24:53; Mart. Carp. 41.

[13] 4 Macc. 18:3 (cf. n. 15). Mart. Pion. 22:1. Mart. Carp. 41 (a prayer). ApCo 8.15.2 (Eucharistic).

[14] Cf. John 12:27. Despite parallels in the liturgies (Brightman, I, 43: "make us *worthy* of this *hour*"), it is unlikely that this once had to do with the hour of the Eucharist rather than with the hour of martyrdom (cf. Reuning p. 38).

[15] 4 Macc. 18:3; Rev. 20:6. Mart. Carp. 41 (a prayer). Origen, *Homilies on Jeremiah* 14.14 (a prayer). But see also *Anaph. Serap.* 16.3: "make us to have a *portion* with the Body and Blood."

[16] Cf. Exod. 12:4; Deut. 32:8; Luke 22:3; Rev. 6:9-11; 7:4; 13:17, 18; 15:2. 1 Clem. 59:2 ("liturgical"). ApCo 8.5.6; 8.22.3 (liturgical).

[17] Perhaps originally Eucharistic. For the Eucharistic "cup" associated with the bestowal of the "Holy Spirit" and "eternal life" see ApCo 8.12.38-39 (cf. Ign. Eph. 20:2; *Anaph. Serap.* 13.15). In the present context the reference is to the cup of martyrdom (Mart. Isa. 5.3; cf. Mark 14:36).

[18] ApCo 8.15.2 (Eucharistic).

[19] Cf. 4 Macc. 15:3; John 5:29. ApCo 8.14.2, "the life of the age to come" (Eucharistic).

[20] ApCo 8.14.2, "to the benefit of soul and body" (Eucharistic).

[21] Cf. 4 Macc. 17:12.

---

less, this particular prayer looks more like a piece of liturgy than *verba ipsissima*. The above parallels indicate that it is at least closely related to the liturgical tradition and may have Eucharistic affinities in particular. There seems to be no clear evidence that elements in the prayer are beyond the range of possibilities in the middle of the second

among whom may I *be received* today *as a rich* and
acceptable *sacrifice*,[22]
just as you have *prepared* beforehand,[23]
and revealed beforehand,
and fulfilled,
O *undeceiving and true God*.[24]

3. For this reason and for all these things *I praise you*,
I bless you,
I glorify you,[25]
through the *eternal and heavenly high priest Jesus Christ*[26]
your *beloved Son*[s]
*through whom to you with him and the Holy Spirit be glory
now and forever*.[27] Amen."

XI. The martyrdom of Polycarp: The burning (15:1–16:2)

15 When he had lifted up the "Amen" and finished the prayer,

---

[22] Cf. Dan. 3:39-40 LXX (a prayer). For Jewish parallels to this conception of the martyr see Fischel, *JQR*, 37 (1946/47), 372-374; note also 2 Macc. 1:24-26; 4 Macc. 1:11; 6:29; 17:22; Ign. Eph. 21:1; Smyrn. 10:2; Polyc. 2:3; 6:1. But in Mart. Polyc. 14:1, 2 the vicarious and/or atoning nature of this sacrifice is hardly hinted at. We seem to be dealing with a conception of the martyr's perfection—the truly acceptable form of sacrifice or gift which a man can offer God (cf. Eusebius, *M.P.* 11.22).

[23] Cf. Did. 10:5 (Eucharistic?). These lines, however, reflect more than any other the particular situation (cf. Mart. Polyc. 5:2).

[24] ApCo 8.18.1 (liturgical; cf. 7.26.3). For "true" cf. John 17:3; Ign. Rom. 8:2.

[25] These terms are biblical; but they are found together like this only in later liturgical prayers: ApCo 7.47.2; Brightman, I, 329 (cf. ApCo 8.13.10). Note also ApCo 8.12.27: *"for all these things* to you be glory."

[26] See Polyc. Phil. 12:2. 1 Clem. 61:3 (cf. ch. 64); ApCo 7.47.2 (liturgical).

[27] See J. A. Robinson, *JTS*, 21 (1920), 101-105; 24 (1923), 141-144 (Connolly, *JTS*, 24 [1923], 144-146), who gives later liturgical parallels and suggests that the "conglorification" of the Spirit is incredible at this early period. J. W. Tyrer, *JTS*, 23 (1922), 390-392, doubts that the form of the doxology is late (cf. Justin, *Apol.* 1.65.3; Clement, *Paed.* 3.101) and in any event accepts Eusebius' (theologically more primitive) reading at this point: "in the Holy Spirit."

---

century. For analyses of parallels and structure see H. Lietzmann, *ZWT*, 54 (1912), 56-61 and Reuning pp. 31-43. The threefold nature of much of the prayer deserves notice.

15:1. *We:* The claim to eyewitness has been vigorously defended

the men attending to the fire lit it. And when a great flame shot up, we, to whom it was given to see, saw a miracle; and we were preserved to tell the rest what happened. 2. For the fire took the form of an arch like the sail of a ship filled by the wind and encircled the body of the martyr like a wall. And he was in the center of it not like burning flesh but like baking bread or like gold and silver being refined in a furnace; for we also perceived a fragrant odor like the scent of incense or some other precious spice.

16 At last when the lawless pagans saw that his body could not be consumed by fire, they ordered the executioner to go up to him and plunge a dagger into him. And when he had done this, [a

---

by Reuning p. 3. Keim p. 108, however, suggests that the verb "preserved" betrays a later perspective; but the author(s) may be alluding simply to the fact that they escaped persecution. *Miracle:* For the (relative) invulnerability of martyrs in Jewish sources see Fischel, *JQR*, 37 (1946/47), 376-377. Martyrdom is also one of the reasons why "the men of old" had miracles done for them (Berakoth 20a). **15:2.** *Not like burning flesh*, etc.: Eusebius (*H.E.* 4.15.37) reads, "not like burning flesh but like gold and silver being refined in a furnace." This is possibly the correct reading. Schwartz's (*De Pionio*, 15) defense of m ("not like burning flesh but like baking bread") depends on a rationalistic effort to account for the smell (differently motivated are Reuning pp. 44-45, and Keim p. 94, n. 1). But when it is recognized that a fragrant odor is related to the presence of sanctity in the history of religions, it is the reference to "baking bread" that seems less natural (cf. E. Lohmeyer, *SHA*, 1919, 46-49). For the transforming effect of fire see 4 Maccabees 9:22; the Martyrdom of Polycarp 2:3 (cf. 1 Pet. 1:7; Rev. 1:15). The "odor of sanctity" became a standard element in the acts of the martyrs (cf. Eusebius, *H.E.* 5.1.35; Mart. Perp. 13.3; Eusebius, *M.P.* 11.27).

16:1. *Dagger:* No parallelism with John 19:34 is intended (we are not even told that the dagger pierced *his side* as we would expect if John were imitated). The *confector* (executioner) is the one "who gave the coup de grace to wounded gladiators" or the wild beasts (BAG, 443). The games had just been concluded (12:2). For a similar treatment of martyrs see Mart. Perp. 21.3. *A dove and:* Omitted by Eusebius (*H.E.* 4.15.39). There is almost universal agreement that this was added later (probably by Ps-Pionius). P. Corssen's defense of the phrase (*ZNW*, 5 [1904], 286) is related to his confidence in the authenticity of Pionius' *Life of Polycarp*. That confidence is misplaced (cf. below, 22:3); moreover, Eusebius would

dove and] a large quantity of blood came out so that it quenched the fire and the whole crowd was amazed that there was so great a difference between unbelievers and the elect. 2. [Of the elect was he indeed one, this most wonderful Polycarp—a man who in our times showed himself an apostolic and prophetic teacher and bishop of the catholic church in Smyrna. For every word that he uttered was fulfilled and will be fulfilled.]

XII. The relics of Polycarp (17:1-18:3)

17 Now when the jealous, envious, and evil one, the enemy of the race of the just, saw that his martyrdom had been illustrious and his life irreproachable from the beginning, that he was

---

hardly have been squeamish about a miraculous element like this (cf. H.E. 6.29.3). Wordworth's emendation (*peri styraka*) is also unnecessary. For the connection in Greece and elsewhere between bird and soul see G. van der Leeuw, *Phänomenologie der Religion* (Tübingen, 1956), 331-332. The dove was the natural choice for Christians (cf. Tertullian, *De Baptismo* 8). Such miracles are common in late martyr acts. 16:2. *Of the elect*, etc.: Eusebius (*H.E.* 4.15.39) omits "Polycarp." Schwartz (*De Pionio*, 16) regards the name as well as "apostolic and prophetic teacher" and the "and" (only in b p) before "bishop" as later additions. But the whole of verse 2 is probably an interpolation (Reuning pp. 21-22; Campenhausen, *SHA*, 1957, 22-23). It is clumsy; it does not seem to be fully in harmony with the context; "in our times" does not suggest a contemporary perspective; the emphasis on the prophetic role of the bishop may be anti-Montanist; "catholic" here seems to be used in the (later) sense of "orthodox," as it is not elsewhere in the Martyrdom of Polycarp (though the reading of m, Lat.—"holy"—may be correct); the "elect" in 16:1 seems to refer to Christians; in 16:2 to martyrs. The majority of MSS read "martyr" after the adjective "most wonderful" and may be right; the title "bishop and martyr" of Polycarp occurs already in Polycrates' letter preserved by Eusebius (*H.E.* 5.24.4); the expression "apostolic and prophetic teacher" reflects a not unheard of evaluation of the bishop as teacher (Hippolytus, *Ref.* Proem, 6) with prophetic gifts (Did. 15:1) exercising apostolic authority (Irenaeus, *Adv. haer.* 3.3.4; 5.20.1; cf. Eusebius, *H.E.* 5.20.7).

17:1-18:3. The attitude of the Smyrnaeans to Polycarp's relics can be understood only (*a*) if the passage—especially 18:3—betrays the perspective of a later generation or (*b*) if it indicates a pattern of thinking already sufficiently familiar to the Church (from within or without) to allow even for the anticipation of an annual celebration. This pattern undeniably reflects (*a*) the Greek cult of the dead, or (*b*)

crowned with the crown of incorruption and had carried off the incontestable prize, he set about preventing even his poor body being taken by us, though there were many who wanted to do this and to have fellowship with his holy flesh. 2. [So he incited Nicetes, the father of Herod and brother of Alce, to beg the magistrate not to give up his body, "Lest," he said, "they abandon the Crucified and begin to worship this man." And this they said at the instigation and urging of the Jews who were also watching when we were about to take him from the fire; they did not know that we shall never find it possible either to abandon Christ who

---

the hero cult, or (c) both. The two were closely related; both centered about the grave, though the cult of heroes was less bound to it (Nilsson, I², 179, 186-191; II, 110-111, 136, 522, 524). Perhaps Delehaye (*Origines*, 24-26) is correct in suggesting that the divine status accorded heroes in our period would have made Christian appropriation of cultus related to them difficult. In any event, the interest in Polycarp's "holy flesh" (17:1; cf. 13:2) and "precious" bones (18:2) presupposes recognition of a peculiar sanctity of godly men found in many forms in many different religious milieus (even the Old Testament: 2 Kings 13:21). This in turn heralds the later emphasis on the miracles of the saint, which is more closely related to the religiosity surrounding the hero (Nilsson, I², 189). It is also at this point that the Jewish interest in the graves of martyr-prophets (Fischel, *JQR*, 37 [1946/47], 374-376) has affinities with Christian hagiography.

Although there is justifiable doubt about the reliability of the text of 17:2-3 (see below), I can see no convincing reason for regarding chapter 18 as an interpolation.

17:1. *Crown of incorruption:* Cf. 4 Macc. 17:12,15; Eusebius, *H.E.* 5.1.36; Lucian, *Peregrinus* 33. *His poor body:* Permission to bury the bodies of executed criminals could be obtained by anyone, according to Roman law. Ulpian, however, says: "hodie . . . nonnumquam non permittitur, *maxime maiestatis causa* damnatorum" (*Dig.* 48.24). Eusebius knows of many cases in which the remains of martyrs were not given up (Lawlor-Oulton, II, 334). Yet in a sense that is not really the case here, since the law takes it for granted that in the case of those condemned to die by burning their "bodies may be requested—that is to say, that their bones and ashes may be collected and deposited in a grave" (*Dig.* 48.24). *Though . . . holy flesh:* Regarded as an interpolation by von Campenhausen (*SHA*, 1957, 29) on insufficient grounds. **17:2.** *So he incited:* Eusebius (*H.E.* 4.15.41) reads "some incited" (to agree with the plural subject of the next sentence); other variants indicate similar difficulties with the text; but the "evil one" seems to be the subject here. Von Campenhausen (*SHA*, 1957, 25-26) regards this as one indication that 17:2-3 is an

THE MARTYRDOM OF POLYCARP 75

suffered for the salvation of those saved in all the world, the blameless for the sinners [cf. 1 Pet. 3:18], or to worship any other. 3. For him we worship as the Son of God; but the martyrs we love as disciples and imitators of the Lord, as they deserve because of their incomparable loyalty to their own King and Teacher. May it also be granted us to become their partners and fellow disciples.]

18 When the centurion, then, saw the contentiousness caused by the Jews, he put him in the center, as they usually do, and burned him. 2. Accordingly, we later took up his bones, more precious than costly stones and finer than gold, and deposited them in a

---

interpolation. He also notes that Nicetes' relationship with Herod is explained for a second time (cf. 8:2); that the mention of Alce (cf. Ign. Smyrn. 13; Polyc. 8:3) looks like the biographical curiosity characteristic of later hagiography; that the "customary" action of the centurion in 18:1 does not presuppose a special directive from the proconsul. *Lest . . . this man:* Conceivable in the mouth of a pagan (or Jew); according to Eusebius, *H.E.* 8.6.7, Christian martyrs in Diocletian's time were exhumed "lest any, regarding them as actually gods (so at least they imagined), should worship them as they lay in their tombs." But this is somewhat abnormal (cf. Eusebius, *H.E.* 5.1.61-63). Moreover, the form of the statement seems to reflect a debate within Christian circles and points forward to the careful distinction made in 17:3 (cf. Eusebius, *H.E.* 5.2.2-4). Excessive veneration of martyrs is probably presupposed. *And this they said:* In the MSS, "they said" is unexpressed; Eusebius (*H.E.* 4.15.41) supplies the verb—more or less correctly it would seem. Those who translate, "he—that is, the devil—said," and refer "they did not know" to the "Jews" strain the syntax with a view to a better logical connection. The confusion supports the theory of interpolation. *Jews:* Their role in early Christian persecutions is slight. Some have conjectured that their presence here is more an aspect of the imitation theme (cf. Matt. 27:36, 64; 28:4) than of history (Simon p. 151). But there is no need to rule out such activity entirely (Rev. 2:9; Justin, *Apol.* 1.31.6; Tertullian, *Scorp.* 10; Eusebius, *H.E.* 5.16.12). The reference here may well be a fragment of the original text which made intelligible the "contentiousness caused by the Jews" of 18:1. 17:2–3. *Worship:* The two words so translated (*sebein, proskynein*) are found together elsewhere in early Christian literature (Justin, *Apol.* 1.6.2; Mart. Carp. 5, 7; Mart. Just. 4.4).

18:2. *In a suitable place:* Cf. Mart. Just. 6.2. 18:3. *Birthday:* The earliest evidence for an annual memorial of the dead. See also Martyrdom of Pionius 2:1-2 (in which Polycarp's "birthday" is again dis-

suitable place. 3. And there, in so far as it is possible, the Lord will grant that we come together with joy and gladness and celebrate the birthday of his martyrdom both in memory of those who have contended in former times and for the exercise and training of those who will do so in the future.

XIII. Conclusion (19:1–20:2)

19 Such is the story of the blessed Polycarp. Although he was martyred in Smyrna along with eleven others from Philadelphia, he alone is indeed remembered by all so that he is spoken of everywhere even by the Gentiles. Not only did he show himself a distinguished teacher but also an outstanding martyr, whose martyrdom all desire to imitate since it was in accord with the

---

cussed) and Tertullian, *De Monogamia* 10 (not of martyrs). For the term "birthday" as standard for the anniversaries of martyrs see *Concilium Laodicenum* 51. The classical guess as to its origin is that it reflected the belief of the early Church that a man's true birth lay before him (cf. Ign. Rom. 6:1; Zahn, *Ignatius*, 560; this is disputed by Delehaye, *Origines*, 35-36). In the Greek cult of the dead a man's (natural) birthday was the most important day of commemoration (Schmidt, PWK, VII, 1137-1138). We are dealing with a Christian transformation of this in the Martyrdom of Polycarp. *Memory:* Cf. 4 Macc. 17:7-10. *Contended:* The verbal form of the noun "athlete." This is a Stoic metaphor (cf. also "crown," "prize," "exercise," "training") occurring already in 4 Macc. 17:11-16; 1 Clem. 5:1-2 with particular reference to martyrdom (cf. Ign. Polyc. 1:3, 2:3, 3:1).

19:1. *Eleven others from Philadelphia:* Presumably discussed in 2:1-3:2 (see p. 57). Perhaps their origin is not mentioned earlier to remove attention from the overcautious behavior of the Smyrnaeans. The Greek reads literally, "Polycarp . . . the twelfth along with those from Philadelphia" (for the construction see B-D, 130; possibly, "eleven others including those from Philadelphia"). There may be some emphasis on the number (cf. Eusebius, *M.P.* 11.li, 11.25; note that the number seven is regarded as significant in 4 Macc. 14:8). Some have thought that Eusebius (*H.E.* 4.15.46) refers to further accounts (or at least the names) of the eleven Philadelphian martyrs when he says, "in the same writing [*graphē*, of Martyrdom of Polycarp in 4.15.2,8,15] concerning him [Polycarp] other martyrdoms as well were subjoined which took place in the same Smyrna about the same period of time with Polycarp's martyrdom." But it seems more likely that Eusebius is referring to a collection of martyr acts (Lawlor-Oulton, II, 136). Thus the summary of the fate of Pionius, which follows, is a mirror of the Martyrdom of Pionius. (Von Campen-

gospel of Christ. 2. Through patience he overcame the unjust magistrate and thus carried off the crown of incorruption; and rejoicing with the apostles and all the just, he is glorifying God and the Father Almighty and is blessing our Lord Jesus Christ, the Savior of our souls, the Helmsman of our bodies, and the Shepherd of the catholic church throughout the world.

20 Now you asked that a detailed report be made to you; for

---

hausen, *SHA*, 1957, 35-36, is forced to assume that Pionius was mentioned in the Martyrdom of Polycarp and that Eusebius used the name as a point of departure for drawing in references to the Martyrdom of Pionius. He further argues that Eusebius' language concerning Metrodorus—he "seemed" to be a Marcionite—indicates that the Martyrdom of Polycarp regarded him as catholic. This, however, is Eusebius' way of grudgingly giving Marcionite heretics their due; cf. *H.E.* 5.16.21; 7.12; *M.P.* 10.3S. Eusebius is simply reflecting Martyrdom of Pionius 21.5-6 where Metrodorus' heresy is acknowledged; he is not reflecting a conflict between the witness of the Martyrdom of Pionius and the Martyrdom of Polycarp.) *He alone . . . indeed*: Schwartz (*De Pionio*, 17) supposes that we have a conflation here of the original reading—*pantōn mallon*—and an old interpolation—*monos hypo*. Our translation of *mallon* depends on a looser patristic use (Lampe p. 825). The MSS of the Martyrdom of Polycarp have dropped it completely. (Schwartz regards the interpolation as prompted by an even earlier interpolation—the clause which makes the "exaggerated" claim that the pagans also recognized Polycarp.) *Gentiles*: Eusebius *H.E.* 4.15.45 ends at this point. This can hardly be used as evidence that he was ignorant of the imitation theme which follows (Campenhausen, *SHA*, 1957, 13-14). Once again Eusebius ignores what does not have to do rather directly with the "story of the beloved Polycarp" (see p. 52) and takes the martyrdom's own remarks at this point as a signal to stop. (That he stops in the middle of a sentence—in the Greek—is not unusual; see Lawlor-Oulton, II, 20-22.) At the same time, it seems most unlikely that Eusebius would have omitted reference to the material contained in our chapter 21 had he known it (though it is possible that he did not know enough about the details to be able to make use of it). We conclude that his copy of the Martyrdom of Polycarp probably ended at the end of 20:2 (which not only has a doxology but a final salutation). **19:2.** *With the apostles*, etc.: The martyrs have a place near God's throne (cf. Rev. 6:9; 20:4, 6; Eusebius, *H.E.* 6.42.5; Cyprian, *Ep.* 6.2; 15.3; 31.3). The further thought that the martyrs alone have *immediate* access to the throne of God does not seem to be present here. In the early church it appears to be found only in Tertullian (*De Anima* 55.4; Campenhausen, *Idee*, 125, n. 8). **20:1.** *Marcion*: The reading of m (probably

the present we have made this summary available through our brother Marcion. When you have absorbed the contents, send the letter on to the brethren farther on so that they too may glorify the Lord who makes election from among his servants.

2. Now to him who is able to bring us all by his grace and favor into his eternal kingdom, through his Son, his only one, Jesus Christ, be glory, honor, power, and majesty forever.

Greet all the saints. Those with us and Evarestus, the scribe, with all his house greet you.

Appendix I (21:1)

21 The blessed Polycarp was martyred on the second day at the beginning of the month of Xanthicus, seven days before the kalends of March, a Great Sabbath, at the eighth hour. He was

---

changed to Marcianus and Marcus in various texts at least in part because of the associations which the name Marcion awakened). Marcion was primarily responsible for the composition of the letter, whereas Evarestus (vs. 2) was the scribe. **20:2.** *The doxology:* Simonetti (*GIF*, 9 [1956], 330) points out that this is a *concluding* doxology. Arguments from Romans 15:30–16:27 to the effect that a writer may use more than one more or less final doxology (thus allowing for the authenticity of at least Mart. Polyc. 21) fail in so far as the doxologies which occur in Paul before the end are only brief utterances of praise. Martyrdom of Polycarp 20:2 is a full doxology akin to that in Romans 16:25-27.

21:1. We have presented our reasons above for regarding this as an addition to the Martyrdom of Polycarp. Conservative criticism has come to grant as much (cf. Marrou, *AB*, 71 [1953], 7-10). There is no way of telling how early an addition it may be; clearly great caution is necessary in using it for dating the martyrdom of Polycarp.

Second . . . of . . . Xanthicus: This month is of Macedonian origin (properly Xandicus). The calendar in which the second of Xanthicus corresponds to "seven days before the kalends of March" (Feb. 23) is found in W. Dittenberger, *Orientis Graeci Inscriptiones Selectae*, II (Leipzig, 1905), 56-58 (No. 458) and Schwartz (*Ostertafeln*, 128). The chronological task is to find a February 23 which satisfies the other requirements made by this chapter. February 23 fell on a Saturday in 155 and 166; and Quadratus' proconsulship is usually dated 154/55 (see below). But the difficulties are not ended. For one thing, it so happens that in leap year the extra day is inserted at the beginning of the month of Xanthicus, and this, as Schwartz argues, leaves the possibility that the martyrdom was celebrated on February 23 but actually took place on February 22 or February 24. Schwartz regards

arrested by Herod, when Philip the Trallian was high priest, and Statius Quadratus proconsul, but our Lord Jesus Christ king forever; to whom be glory, honor, majesty, and an eternal throne from generation to generation. Amen.

the "Great Sabbath" as having to do with the Passover (cf. John 19:31; Lightfoot suggested Purim to account for the early date)—that is, with the full moon. Astronomical tables assist in finding a Saturday, near a full moon, on or about February 23. But February 23, 155, does not satisfy the requirements (no full moon). Thus Schwartz opts for February 22, 156. Such arguments probably take the "Great Sabbath" more seriously than is justifiable (cf. 8:1). *Eighth hour:* About two hours after noon (Cadoux pp. 359, 363, n. 1). Possibly deduced from 12:2. Codex m reads "ninth hour," in imitation of Matthew 27:46. *Philip the Trallian:* Hardly to be distinguished from the Asiarch of 12:2 (Cadoux p. 356, n. 1), though it must be admitted that there is no independent evidence of the identity of the titles Asiarch and high priest (but see Lightfoot, III, 407-411). The name of Gaius Julius Philippus occurs in Trallian inscriptions (*CIG* [Boeckh], 2932, 2933), and an Olympian inscription (A.D. 149) cited by Lightfoot (I, 629) refers to him both as Asiarch and as a Trallian. Our editor seems to be in touch with sound information not contained in 12:2. *Statius Quadratus:* Usually identified with L. Statius Quadratus (consul 142), whose proconsulship in Asia is dated (A.D. 154/55) with the help of complex data supplied in the orations of Aristides (P. Corssen, *ZNW*, 3 [1902], 61-82). R. Syme (*Revue des études anciennes*, 61 [1959], 310-311), however, argues that such a date "postulated an abnormally short lapse of time—twelve years—between the consulate and the proconsulate of Asia." Eusebius' date (A.D. 166/67 [*Chronicon*, ed. Helm (1956), 205]) for Polycarp's martyrdom, on the other hand, is too late for Quadratus' proconsulship (the consular *fasti* have a nineteen-year interval as the maximum between consulate and proconsulate). Völter pp. 2-4 accepts the emendation "Urinatius" for "Statius" to support Westberg's ingenious defense of the date 167; cf. Harrison pp. 276-277 (A. Avillius Urinatius Quadratus was consul in 156). This is hardly convincing (nor is there any evidence that Urinatius was ever proconsul in Asia). We have suggested above (see on 12:2) that the reference to Philip as Asiarch holds us to the sixth decade of the second century; at the same time we must also remember that Polycarp visited Anicetus of Rome (Eusebius, *H.E.* 4.14.1-8), whose accession seems to have taken place in A.D. 155 at the very earliest (Lawlor-Oulton, II, 44); consequently Polycarp's martyrdom would fall between, say, A.D. 155 and 160. If, however, we not only reject the authenticity of chapter 21 but also discount the reference to Philip in 12:2, Eusebius' date or one early in the reign of Marcus Aurelius (A.D. 161–180) may be accepted. See also on chapter 4.

Appendix II (22:1)

22 We pray you fare well, brethren, as you walk by the word of Jesus Christ which is in accord with the gospel. Together with him be glory to God and the Father and the Holy Spirit unto the salvation of the holy elect, even as the blessed Polycarp suffered martyrdom, in whose footsteps may we be found in the kingdom of Jesus Christ.

Appendix IIIA (22:2)

2. Gaius transcribed this from the papers of Irenaeus, who in turn was a disciple of Polycarp. He lived in the same city as Irenaeus. I, Socrates, wrote it out in Corinth from the copies of Gaius. Grace be with you all.

Appendix IIIB (22:3)

3. And I, Pionius, in turn wrote it out from the copy mentioned above after a search made because the blessed Polycarp had showed it to me in a revelation, as I shall explain in the sequel. I

22:1. This appendix is missing in the Latin version (for the evidence of m see below). It appears to present itself as a conclusion to the book; but there can be no doubt that it is an addition (see on 20:2). The presence here of language associated with the imitation theme—"in accord with the gospel"—need not be taken as further evidence that its appearance in 1:1 is secondary. It is more likely that our editor hit upon this as a device to round off the letter.

22:2. Clearly a separate appendix. It makes no claim to be part of the original. The effort to put even the copying of the letter in a sort of succession extending back to Polycarp is disquieting, and suggests that this appendix was reformulated (or even invented) by the editor who appended 22:3. By "Gaius" the reader may have been expected to recall the "churchman" of that name referred to by Eusebius, *H.E.* 2.25.6 (cf. Lawlor-Oulton, II, 208). Grégoire (*Persécutions*, 159-160) even argues that "Socrates"—that is, "Isocrates" (see the Moscow epilogue, 5)—is a corruption of "Quadratus" (which in Greek uncials are not unlike one another), and that this is further evidence of the editor's quest for the names of more or less important personages.

22:3. This appendix brings us down to the lifetime of that Pionius, who, according to the Martyrdom of Pionius 2.1 and 23 was martyred in the days of Decius (contrast Eusebius, *H.E.* 4.15.46; cf. Marrou, *AB*, 71 [1953], 12, n. 3). The expression "as I shall explain in the sequel" suggests that our MSS were once part of a *corpus*

gathered it together, now almost worn out with age, that the Lord Jesus Christ might also gather me together with his elect into his heavenly kingdom. To whom be glory with the Father and the Holy Spirit forever. Amen.

Appendix IV: The Moscow epilogue

1. Gaius transcribed this from the writings of Irenaeus. He lived in the same city as Irenaeus, who in turn was a disciple of the holy Polycarp. 2. Now this Irenaeus was in Rome at the time of the martyrdom of bishop Polycarp and taught many there. Many excellent and altogether sound writings are in circulation in which he mentions Polycarp and recalls that he was instructed by him. He masterfully refuted every heresy and handed on the ecclesiastical and catholic rule of faith as he had received it from the saint. 3. And he also reports this: Once Marcion—the founder of the so-called Marcionites—met the holy Polycarp and said, "Recognize us, Polycarp." The latter replied to Marcion, "I recognize—I recognize the first-born of Satan!" 4. And this is also recorded in the writings of Irenaeus: On the day and at the hour

---

Polycarpianum. Presumably the *Life of Polycarp* written by Pionius (this is not stated but only conjectured) was to follow (though it must further be conjectured that the "revelation" referred to here has been lost from the beginning of that document); the *Life,* in turn, indicates that a list of the leaders of the Smyrnaean church, Polycarp's letter to the Philippians, and possibly also an account of Polycarp's exegesis were parts of the collection. Many believe that this Pionius is a mask for a writer working in the fourth century. Whether this is so or not, depends in large measure on the authenticity of the *Life* (assuming that there is a link between it and the appendix 22:3). Powerful voices have been raised in its defense (Schwartz, *De Pionio,* 24-32; P. Corssen, *ZNW,* 5 [1904], 266-302; Cadoux pp. 306-310), but this view seems forced (Delehaye, *Genres,* 42-57; C. Schmidt, *Gespraeche Jesu mit seinem Juengern nach der Auferstehung* [Leipzig, 1919], 705-725). We conclude that we are probably dealing here with a fourth-century writer masquerading as the martyr Pionius.

The Moscow MS (m) breaks off before the doxology of chapter 21 and adds this special appendix at that point. Presumably it came into existence after the Martyrdom of Polycarp and the *Life of Polycarp* had become separated (the "as I shall explain in the sequel" [22:3] is missing). It is clearly secondary. (For example, what has the appearance of two appendixes in 22:2-3 is worked up into one. The "I, Socrates" of 22:2 is reported here in the third person, which is natural

when Polycarp suffered martyrdom in Smyrna, Irenaeus—who was in the city of Rome—heard a voice like that of a trumpet proclaiming, "Polycarp has suffered martyrdom."

5. So then Gaius, as was stated above, transcribed this from these writings of Irenaeus, and Isocrates transcribed it in Corinth from the copies of Gaius. I, Pionius, in turn wrote it out from the copies of Isocrates, after a search made because of a revelation of the holy Polycarp. I gathered it together, now almost worn out with age, that the Lord Jesus Christ might also gather me together with his elect into his heavenly kingdom. To whom be glory with the Father and the Son and the Holy Spirit forever. Amen.

---

enough, whereas the reverse is hardly credible. The consistent use of "the holy"—that is, "saint"—Polycarp points to a later stage in the use of titles for martyrs.)

1. *Writings:* The editor seems to suggest that it was to be found in Irenaeus' own works. This represents an improbable interpretation of 22:2. 2. *Recalls:* Cf. *Adv. haer.* 3.3.4; Eusebius, *H.E.* 5.20.6. *The ecclesiastical and catholic rule:* The language here is close to the *Life of Polycarp* 12 which may indicate contact with that document. The doxology of the Moscow appendix (vs. 5) and the doxology of the *Life* (ch. 31) also agree in the curious double reference to the Son. 3. *Marcion:* See on Polycarp to the Philippians 7:1. 4. *A voice like that of a trumpet:* In view of what appears to be the truth about the epilogue as a whole, it is bold indeed to use this passage to support Grégoire's late date for the Martyrdom of Polycarp (P. Orgels, *AB*, 69 [1951], 24-25). For Irenaeus' visit to Rome see Eusebius, *H.E.* 5.4.1-2.

SELECTED BIBLIOGRAPHY

(Books or articles marked * are usually cited only by the author's name)

BADEN, H., "Das Polykarpmartyrium," *Pastor Bonus* 24 (1911/12), 705-713; 25 (1912/13), 71-81, 136-151.
*BRIGHTMAN, F. E., *Liturgies Eastern and Western*, Vol. I: *Eastern Liturgies*. Oxford, 1896.
BROX, N., *Zeuge und Märtyrer: Untersuchungen zur frühchristlichen Zeugnis-Terminologie* (Studien zum alten und neuen Testament, Vol. V). Munich, 1961.
*CADOUX, C. J., *Ancient Smyrna: A History of the City from the Earliest Times to 324 A.D.* Oxford, 1948.
CAMPENHAUSEN, H. F. VON, *Die Idee des Martyriums in der alten Kirche*. Göttingen, 1936.
———, *Bearbeitungen und Interpolationen des Polykarpmartyriums* (Sitzungsberichte der Heidelberger Akademie der Wissenschaften: Philosophisch-historische Klasse," Jahrgang 1957, 3. Abhandlung). Heidelberg, 1957. (Abbreviation: *SHA*, 1957.)
CORSSEN, P., "Das Todesjahr Polykarps," *Zeitschrift für die neutestamentliche Wissenchaft* 3 (1902), 61-82.
———, "Die Vita Polycarpi," *Zeitschrift für die neutestamentliche Wissenschaft* 5 (1904), 266-302.
DELEHAYE, H., *Les passions des martyrs et les genres littéraires*. Brussels, 1921.
———, *Sanctus: Essai sur le culte des saints dans l'antiquité* (Subsidia Hagiographica, Vol. XVII). Brussels, 1927.
———, *Les origines du culte des martyrs* (Subsidia Hagiographica, Vol. XX). 2d ed. Brussels, 1933.
FISCHEL, H. A., "Martyr and Prophet," *Jewish Quarterly Review* 37 (1946/47), 265-280, 363-386.
GEBHARDT, O. VON, *Ausgewählte Märtyrerakten*. Berlin, 1902.
GEFFCKEN, J., "Die christlichen Martyrien," *Hermes* 45 (1910), 481-505.
GRÉGOIRE, H., and ORGELS, P., "La véritable date du martyre de S. Polycarpe," *Analecta Bollandiana* 69 (1951), 1-38.
GRÉGOIRE, H., et al., *Les persécutions dans l'empire Romain* (Académie royale de Belgique: classe des lettres et des sciences morales et politiques: mémoires, 1st ed., Vol. XLVI/1; 2d ed. rev., Vol. LVI/5). Brussels, 1951, 1964.
*HARRISON, P. N., *Polycarp's Two Epistles to the Philippians*. Cambridge, Eng., 1936.

HELM, R., *Eusebius Werke*, Vol. VII: *Die Chronik des Hieronymus* (*Die griechischen christlichen Schriftsteller der ersten drei Jahrhunderte*). 2d ed. Berlin, 1956.
*HOLL, K., "Die Vorstellung vom Märtyrer und die Märtyrerakte in ihrer geschichtlichen Entwicklung," in *Gesammelte Aufsätze zur Kirchengeschichte*, II (Tübingen, 1928), 68-102.
*KEIM, TH., *Aus dem Urchristenthum*. Vol. I. Zurich, 1878.
KLEIST, J. A., *The Didache, The Epistle of Barnabas, The Epistles and the Martyrdom of St. Polycarp, The Fragments of Papias, The Epistle to Diognetus* (*Ancient Christian Writers*, Vol. VI). Westminster, Md., 1961. (Abbreviation: ACW, VI.)
KNOPF, R., *Ausgewählte Märtyrerakten* (*Sammlung ausgewählter Kirchen- und Dogmengeschichtlicher Quellenschriften*, N.F. Vol. III). 3d ed. rev. G. Krueger. Tübingen, 1929.
KRÜGER, G., *Die Rechtsstellung der vorkonstantinischen Kirchen* (*Kirchenrechtliche Abhandlungen*, Vols. CXV-CXVI). Stuttgart, 1935.
*LAMPE, G. W. H. (ed.), *A Patristic Greek Lexicon*. Oxford, 1961-.
*LAWLOR, H. J., and OULTON, J. E. L., *Eusebius, Bishop of Caesarea: The Ecclesiastical History and the Martyrs of Palestine*. 2 vols. London, 1954.
LIETZMANN, H., "Ein liturgisches Bruchstück des Zweiten Jahrhunderts," *Zeitschrift für wissenschaftliche Theologie* 54 (1912), 56-61.
*LIGHTFOOT, J. B., *The Apostolic Fathers*, Part II: *S. Ignatius, S. Polycarp*. 3 vols. 2d ed. rev. London, 1889.
LOHMEYER, E., *Vom göttlichen Wohlgeruch* (*Sitzungsberichte der Heidelberger Akademie der Wissenschaften: Philosophisch-historische Klasse*, Vol. X/9). Heidelberg, 1919. (Abbreviation: SHA, 1919.)
MARROU, H.-I., "La date du martyre de S. Polycarpe," *Analecta Bollandiana* 71 (1953), 5-20.
MEINHOLD, P., "Polykarpos," in *Paulys Realencyclopädie der classischen Altertumswissenschaft*, ed. G. Wissowa and W. Kroll, XXI/2 (Stuttgart, 1952), 1662-1693. (Abbreviation: PWK, XXI.)
MOMMSEN, TH., *Römisches Staatsrecht* (*Handbuch der römischen Alterthümer*). 2d ed. Vol. II. Leipzig, 1877.
———, "Der Religionsfrevel nach römischen Recht," *Historische Zeitschrift* 64 (1890), 389-429.
———, *Römisches Strafrecht* (*Systematisches Handbuch der deutschen Rechtswissenschaft*). Leipzig, 1899.
MÜLLER, H., *Aus der Ueberlieferungsgeschichte des Polykarp-Martyrium: Eine hagiographische Studie*. Paderborn, 1908.
———, "Das Martyrium Polycarpi: ein Beitrag zur altchristlichen Heiligengeschichte," *Römische Quartalschrift* 22 (1908), 1-16.

*MUSURILLO, H. A., *The Acts of the Pagan Martyrs: Acta Alexandrinorum*. Oxford, 1954.
*NAUTIN, P., *Lettres et écrivains chrétiens des IIe et IIIe siècles* (Patristica, Vol. II). Paris, 1961.
*NILSSON, M. P., *Geschichte der griechischen Religion* (Handbuch der Altertumswissenschaft). Vol. I (2d ed.); Munich, 1955. Vol. II (1st ed.); Munich, 1950.
PERLER, O., "Das vierte Makkabäerbuch, Ignatius von Antiochien und die ältesten Martyrerberichte," *Rivista di Archeologia Cristiana* 25 (1949), 47-72.
*RAMSAY, W. M., *The Church in the Roman Empire Before A.D. 170*. 3d ed. London, 1894.
*REUNING, W., *Zur Erklärung des Polykarpmartyriums*. Darmstadt, 1917.
SCHMIDT, C., *Gespräche Jesu mit seinem Jüngern nach der Auferstehung* (Texte und Untersuchungen, Vol. XLIII). Leipzig, 1919.
SCHWARTZ, E., *Christliche und jüdische Ostertafeln* (Abhandlungen der königlichen Gesellschaft der Wissenschaft zu Göttingen: Philologisch-historische Klasse, N. F. Vol. VIII/6). Berlin, 1905. (Abbreviation: *Ostertafeln*.)
———, *De Pionio et Polycarpo*. Göttingen, 1905.
*SHERWIN-WHITE, A. N., *Roman Society and Roman Law in the New Testament*. Oxford, 1963.
*SILD, O., *Das altchristliche Martyrium in Berücksichtigung der rechtlichen Grundlage der Christenverfolgung*. Dorpat, 1920.
*SIMON, M., *Verus Israel: étude sur les relations entre chrétiens et juifs dans l'empire Romain* (Bibliothèque des écoles françaises d'Athènes et de Rome, Vol. CLXVI.) Paris, 1948.
SIMONETTI, M., "Alcune Osservazioni sul Martirio di S. Policarpo," *Giornale Italiano di Filologia* 9 (1956), 328-344.
*SURKAU, H.-W., *Martyrien in jüdischer und frühchristlicher Zeit*. Göttingen, 1938.
TELFER, W., "The Date of the Martyrdom of Polycarp," *Journal of Theological Studies*, N.S. 3 (1952), 79-83.
*TORRANCE, T. F., *The Doctrine of Grace in the Apostolic Fathers*. Grand Rapids, Mich., 1948.
*VÖLTER, D., *Die apostolischen Väter, neu untersucht*, Vol. II/2: *Polycarp und Ignatius und die ihnen zugeschriebenen Briefe*. Leiden, 1910.
*WEISS, J., *Earliest Christianity: A History of the Period A.D. 30-150*. New York, 1959.
*ZAHN, TH., *Ignatii et Polycarpi Epistulae, Martyria, Fragmenta* (Patrum Apostolicorum Opera, Vol. II). 3d ed. Leipzig, 1876.

THE FRAGMENTS OF PAPIAS

THE FRAGMENTS OF PAPIAS

Introduction

Irenaeus (*Adv. haer.* 5.33.4)—and Eusebius before writing his *Ecclesiastical History* (*Chronicon,* ed. Helm [1956], 193-194, 412-413)—regarded Papias and Polycarp as companions of one another and hearers of John the apostle. Conservative scholarship has usually accepted these claims and has sought to interpret the fragments of Papias accordingly. It is the authorship of the Fourth Gospel, of course, which is primarily at stake. To many it appears that there is no evidence in the fragments of a link between the apostle John and Papias and that Irenaeus was mistaken. Some, however, think that Papias did accept Johannine authorship of the Fourth Gospel (and Revelation) but was not himself in contact with the apostle. In this connection it has been suggested that Papias dated the Fourth Gospel (and Revelation) very early.

These problems will be discussed in the commentary. Here, however, a few preliminary remarks are in order. In one passage Irenaeus advances the view that John lived in Asia until the days of Trajan, and there links the statement with tradition derived from the "elders" (*Adv. haer.* 2.22.5; see p. 127). Such tradition, as we shall see, may well go back to Papias (Loofs pp. 310-338). The question, then, is whether this remark about the apostle John represents an addition of Irenaeus to (or misunderstanding of) his source. Loofs p. 320 thinks not. His argument runs as follows: The same view is advanced in similar terms also in *Adv. haer.* 3.3.4; there it does not quite fit the context; therefore it represents material that has been drawn from a source; in light of *Adv. haer.* 2.22.5, that source is the "elders"—that is, Papias. But the claim that the statement in *Adv. haer* 3.3.4 does not quite fit the context is unfounded. It depends on the grammatical argument that the pronoun *autois* (masculine plural) could not refer to *hē en Ephesō ekklēsia* (feminine singular). Such a construction according to the sense of the passage (*ad sententiam*), however, is not at all unusual in Greek. See Kühner-Gerth, *Ausführliche Grammatik der griechischen Sprache*, II/1 (Hanover, 1898), 54.

It is more likely that Irenaeus is responsible for this element in the tradition of the elders and that he deduced his views on the matter from Papias. He may have regarded John the elder and John the apostle (Eusebius, *H.E.* 3.39.3-4) as one and the same person. Since the former is an important source of Papias (Eusebius, *H.E.* 3.39.7), it was natural to think that Papias was a hearer of the apostle. As we see it, Papias does seem to say in his prologue that the "elders" were disciples of the apostles. To that extent Irenaeus is probably correct in the interpretation of his source (cf. *Adv. haer.* 5.5.1: "the elders, disciples of the apostles"). But the fragments do not seem to lend support to the extension of this view, which sees in John the apostle a particularly important (and long-lived) link in the chain of tradition at Ephesus and a personal acquaintance of Papias.

The link between Polycarp and John, then, is hardly less artificial. Certainly the former's letter to the Philippians leaves no impression of any such direct contact. To be sure, Irenaeus who saw Polycarp suggests the contrary (Eusebius, *H.E.* 4.14.3; 5.20.5). But however long one stretches out the time in which Irenaeus and Polycarp may have known each other (cf. Zahn, *Forschungen*, VI, 27-40), the fact remains that Irenaeus' information on Polycarp is thin indeed (cf. *Adv. haer.* 3.3.4).

If Polycarp and Papias were in any sense "companions," they could not have drunk long from the same theological springs. Polycarp speaks like the Pastorals, whereas Papias ignores Paul, seeks out sayings of the Lord, reflects on the fulfillment of Old Testament promises, shows contact with Rabbinic exegesis, and sets all this within the framework of a vigorous chiliasm. It would be wrong to deny common ground to the various representatives of Asia Minor Christianity known to us; but it would be equally wrong to speak of a "school of John" if the term "school" has anything like its ordinary weight. Thus the fact that Papias and John's Gospel refer to Christ as "the Truth" has about the same significance as the fact that Revelation and John's Gospel refer to Christ as "the Word." (I assume that Revelation and John represent two rather distinct theological orientations.) Similarly, the fact that Polycarp shares with 1 John an anti-Docetic polemic does not necessarily mean that the underlying structure of their thought is the same.

Papias was bishop of Hierapolis in Phrygia (Eusebius, H.E. 3.36.1-2), a city located near the meeting point of two important roads—that running from Antioch (in Syria) to Ephesus and that running from Attalia (in Pamphylia) to Smyrna. The name "Papias" was particularly common in Phrygia (W. H. P. Hatch, ZNW, 12 [1911], 83), and this may indicate that our author was a native of the region. It may also have been in Hierapolis that he picked up the rhetorical skills which he displays. For the cities of Asia Minor provided livelihoods for numerous rhetoricians in this period.

Dates for Papias' writing have ranged all the way from late in the first century (see especially E. Gutwenger, *Zeitschrift für katholische Theologie*, 69 [1947], 385-416) to past the middle of the second century (Harnack). Eusebius deals with Papias together with Ignatius and Polycarp in the reign of Trajan. It seems that if Eusebius pushed Papias' date in any direction, it would be later rather than earlier in order to banish chiliasm from the primitive period; at the same time, it is possible that he dated him too early under the influence of Irenaeus, who sought to find as early a witness as possible to chiliastic thinking! In any event, Papias knew the Gospels of Mark, Matthew, and (probably) John, and the letters of 1 Peter and 1 John. It is uncertain, as we shall see, whether he knew Revelation. At the other extreme, we know that Papias' work was used by Irenaeus—some think already by Justin (cf. Bacon pp. 439-442). I understand Papias' prologue to claim knowledge of apostolic tradition primarily through those who had known elders who in turn were in contact with the apostles. That is vague from a chronological point of view, especially since geographical as well as chronological distance may play a role. But it seems to rule out the earliest dates which reckon with the possibility of direct contact between Papias and the apostles. At the same time, Gnosticism does not yet seem to pose a significant threat to the Christianity known to Papias (at least as I understand the fragments); he can still ignore Paul (apparently); he can deal with evangelic tradition in a way that reminds us of the freedom of most of the Apostolic

Fathers in this respect. This is all very unsatisfactory; but I can see no reason to refuse to allow Eusebius' date to stand and would agree with Bartlet (in *Amicitiae Corolla*, 21-22; *DCG*, II, 311) in setting the writing of Papias *ca.* A.D. 110.

Other points bearing on this issue are dealt with in the commentary. It may be noted here that the dating of the martyrdom of Papias along with Polycarp and others in the *Chronicon Paschale* rests on a misreading of Eusebius, *H.E.* 4.15 (Lightfoot, *Essays*, 147-149).

Our translation follows the selection of fragments and text of Karl Bihlmeyer, *Die apostolischen Vaeter: Neubearbeitung der Funkschen Ausgabe*, rev. Wilhelm Schneemelcher, I (Tübingen: J. C. B. Mohr [Paul Siebeck], 1956), 133-140.* Other references to Papias occur in ancient sources (cf. J. B. Lightfoot and J. R. Harmer, *The Apostolic Fathers* [London, 1898], 515-524; E. Preuschen, *Antilegomena* [Giessen, 1905], 91-99; the fragment identified by J. Sykutris, *ZNW*, 26 [1927], 210-212, is hardly authentic, as was shown by G. Goetz, *ZNW*, 27 [1928], 348) but they seem to be of negligible value. References to most of these occur in relevant contexts of the commentary. We shall also draw attention to patterns of thought—particularly in Irenaeus and Victorinus—which seem to have something to do with Papias. For Irenaeus see p. 127. The clearest use of Papias by Victorinus occurs in his *Commentary on Revelation* 4.4 (on Mark) and 21.6 (on the millennium). It is at least certain that the information on Mark was not derived from Eusebius since Victorinus died in A.D. 304. There is a good chance, then, that he or a source had direct contact with the works of Papias. Bartlet (in *Amicitiae Corollae*, 41-44) has a discussion of the possible dependence of elements in Hippolytus on Papias (cf. Zahn, *Forschungen*, VI, 128, n. 2), but it is too tenuous to concern us in this study. He is probably right, however, when he says that "there is yet much unidentified 'Papias' scattered in later Patristic writings."

* I have been unable to find a copy of M. Buccellato, *Papias di Hierapoli: Frammenti e testimonianze nel testo greco* (1936).

Outline

Introduction
I. Creation renewed and liberated
IIA. The prologue
IIB. Extraordinary accounts
IIC. The thousand years
IID. Papias' sources
III. Judas
IV. The fall of Satan
V. The trustworthiness of Revelation
VI. The six days
VII. Paradise
VIII. Children
IX. Enjoyment of food in the resurrection
X. Enjoyment of certain material food
XI. An epitome of Papias' work
XII. The martyrdom of John
XIII. The Gospel of John

The Traditions of the Elders

Introduction
I. The age of Christ
II. Paradise
III. The number 666
IV. Creation renewed and liberated
V. The heavenly rooms
VI. Steps of salvation
VII. Faith
VIII. The concord and tranquility of the animals

The Fragments of Papias

Translation and Commentary

I. Creation renewed and liberated (Irenaeus, *Adv. haer.* 5.33.3-4; cf. Eusebius, *H.E.* 3.39.1)

1. [The blessings of Gen. 27:28-29 refer to the time] when creation, renewed and liberated, will bear an abundance of every kind of food "from the dew of heaven and the fertility of the earth"; thus the elders who saw John, the disciple of the Lord, recalled having heard from him how the Lord used to teach concerning those times and say:

This tradition is traced by Irenaeus to "the elders" of Asia Minor. He seems to have derived it from Papias; at least there is no sign that he had personal contact with these elders. Thus "Papias . . . also" in sec. 4 means that "not only did [the elders] witness the fact, but also Papias has consigned their testimony to writing" (J. Chapman, *JTS*, 9 [1908], 57, against Zahn, *Forschungen*, VI, 88-90).

The context in Irenaeus (*Adv. haer.* 5.33.1-5) may show us the pattern followed by Papias in his *Exposition* (cf. Eusebius, *H.E.* 3.39): (*a*) an "oracle" of Christ, (*b*) an interpretation of it, (*c*) an illustrative story from oral tradition (Lightfoot, *Essays*, 158-159). In this case the "oracle" is Matthew 26:27-29 (note: the "fruit of the vine"); a close parallel to *Adv. haer.* 5.33.3-4 in Victorinus (*Commentary on Revelation* 21.6) is likewise based on Matthew 26:29; and Victorinus is linked (directly?), as we shall see, with Papias also on other grounds.

The tradition is dependent on Jewish apocalyptic ideas. Especially close parallels are provided by 2 Baruch 29:5-6 and 1 Enoch 10:19. Papias' form of the tradition, however, represents a later more elaborate stage in the development of the theme (L. Gry, *Vivre et Penser*, 3 [1944], 112-124; *Revue Biblique*, 53 [1946], 197-206). The midrashic nature of the text is also clear: (*a*) 2 Baruch and Papias both seem to derive the number ten thousand from Genesis 27:28 (quoted by Irenaeus)—"plenty of grain and wine"—by reading *rb*, "plenty," as *rbw*, "ten thousand" (R. Harris). (*b*) "Take me" in Papias (sec. 3) is derived, as Gry had noted, from Genesis 49:12 by taking *hklyly*, "(shall be) dull (red?)," as *ḥky ly ly*, "take (literally, wait for) me,

2. "The days will come
   when vineyards shall grow
      each with ten thousand vines,
      and on one vine ten thousand branches,
      and on one branch ten thousand shoots,
      and on every shoot ten thousand clusters,
      and in every cluster ten thousand grapes,
      and every grape when pressed will give twenty-five
                                              measures of wine;
3. and when one of the saints grasps a cluster,
   another cluster will cry out:
      'I am better,
      take me,
      bless the Lord on my account.'
Similarly a grain of wheat will bring forth ten thousand ears,
   and every ear will have ten thousand grains,
   and every grain ten pounds of clean white flour.
And all the other fruits and seeds and grass
   will bring forth in like proportion.
And all the animals using foods
   which are produced by the earth
   will live peacefully and harmoniously together
   fully subject to men."
4. Papias, a man of the primitive period, who was a hearer of John and a companion of Polycarp, also bears witness to these things in writing in the fourth of his books; for he is the author of five books. And he went on to say:

---

me"; R. Dimi (*Ketuboth* 111b) also uses Genesis 49:12 of the age to come and has a similar play on the word "red" (every *chyk*, "palate," that tastes will say, "To me, to me"). Genesis 27:28 and 49:12 were linked for two reasons: (*a*) both are blessings predicting future glory, (*b*) both contain the word "wine."

For the peace among the animals see Isaiah 11:6-9; 65:25, cited by Irenaeus, *Adv. haer.* 5.33.4.

Beyschlag (*TU*, LXXIX, 269-270) argues that the exchange between Jesus and Judas recalls a Gnostic epiphany scene in which paradise is shown the disciples; but that the account was set by Papias in a new context and thus transformed. Beyschlag offers parallels, however, from the Gospels as well as (later) Gnostic literature; and it is artificial to assume that Papias' ultimate source reflects only the

"These things are credible to those who believe. And," he says, "when Judas the traitor did not believe and asked, 'How then will such extraordinary growths be brought about by the Lord?' the Lord said, 'Those who are alive when they take place will see them.'"

IIA. The prologue (Eusebius, *H.E.* 3.39.1-7)

1. There are five books of Papias in circulation which have the title of "An Exposition of Dominical Oracles." Irenaeus also

---

supposed Gnostic stream lying behind the NT. Moreover, there is a tolerably good parallel to just such doubt concerning the miraculous fruitfulness of the age to come in the case of a "certain disciple" of R. Gamaliel (*Shabbath* 30b).

Gry's theory that this chiliasm represents an interpolation into the work of Papias is based especially on remarkable coincidences between the names of the early Christian fathers involved—Papias, disciple of John—and Jewish authorities—R. Pappos, connected with R. Johanan; R. Dimi, moreover, whom we have already met, is said to have been in charge particularly of R. Johanan's sayings. We are to imagine Jewish tradition becoming confused with the sentiments of Papias.

The connection, however, between R. Pappos and R. Johanan is quite indirect in the Rabbinic sources. The NT Revelation, moreover, makes it clear that millennial thoughts were not unusual in Asian Christianity. In any event, Papias' writing in the form before Irenaeus was profoundly interpenetrated by them—especially if, as seems likely, the traditions of the "elders" known to Irenaeus were mediated to him through Papias' work (see p. 127). Loofs pp. 329-338 has further argued that whole sentences and more in Irenaeus, *Adv. haer.* 5.25-36, even when not directly attributed to the elders, may well go back to Papias. In this connection (pp. 334-338) he suggests that Papias and the elders believed the millennial reign of Christ on earth to be *eternal* (though some progress beyond it) connecting it (cf. *Adv. haer.* 5.30.4; 5.32.2) with the promise of the land to Abraham (as did Victorinus, *Commentary on Revelation* 21.1-2); and that Irenaeus brought this into harmony with the view of Revelation only with difficulty (cf. *Adv. haer.* 5.35.2-36.1-3).

Hippolytus (*Commentary on Daniel* 4.60) echoes, in a somewhat different (and apparently independent) form, the exchange between Judas and Jesus as reported by Papias.

1. For the title of Papias' book one MS reads: "Expositions of Dominical Oracles" (see also fragment IX). This represents an effort to deal with the clumsy genitive *exēgēseōs*. The latter, however, is

makes mention of these as though they were his only writings somewhat as follows: "Papias, a man of the primitive period, who was a hearer of John and a companion of Polycarp, bears witness to these things in writing in the fourth of his books; for he is the author of five books" [Irenaeus, *Adv. haer.* 5.33.4, above]. 2. Such are Irenaeus' words; nevertheless, Papias himself shows in the prologue to his own discourses that he had never been a listener or eyewitness of the sacred apostles but teaches through the expressions he uses that he received the traditions of the faith from those who were familiar with them:

3a. "I shall not hesitate
all that I thoroughly learned from the elders

---

intelligible if it is understood to depend on "five books"—a not unusual thing in the title of Greek books. Lexicographical studies (H. J. Lawlor, *Hermathena*, 43 [1922], 170-197; J. Donovan, *Logia*, 9-40; Hommes pp. 230-249) show that in the relevant literature (*a*) *exēgēsis* means mainly translation or interpretation (the former clearly does not apply here), (*b*) *kyriakos* normally has reference to the Lord Jesus, (*c*) *logia* means oracles, is most often applied to Scripture (first OT; later NT), and has reference (as in 39.15 below) to words and deeds of Jesus. No support can be found for seeing in Papias' five books (as did R. Harris, Burkitt, Gregory, Hatch, and others) an exposition of OT prophecies about Jesus (cf. Lawlor, *Hermathena*, 43 [1922], 198-204; Hommes pp. 225-255). On the other hand, others go too far in virtually equating *logia* and the Gospels (as Scripture). It is true that the Gospels are in fact Papias' prime source, as we shall see, but the term *logia* still puts emphasis on the divinity of the spoken and authoratative word of God (cf. 1 Clem. 19:1; Justin, *Dial.* 18) even when they were felt to coincide with Scripture (see on Polyc. Phil. 7:1). Only in later usage does *logia* fully harden into the sense "Scripture," especially as applied to the NT (e.g., Pseudo-Dionysius, *De Caelesti Hierarchia* 2.2). It is unlikely that Papias discussed all of Christ's sayings as reported in one or more of the Gospels; but nothing can be made of the absence of the definite article in the title. A phrase in Irenaeus, *Adv. haer.* 1. Praef. 1 may reflect the title; but this hardly suffices to show that Papias' work was anti-Gnostic. Papias' five books may have had something to do with the five blocks of sayings of Jesus in Matthew; but other models were available (e.g., the Pentateuch) if one is required at all (see also Eusebius, *H.E.* 4.8.2). It is tenuous in the extreme to see a connection with the collection of OT testimonies in five books by the monk Matthew in a mediaeval MS from Athos (cf. Hommes pp. 21-25).

3-4. The translation of this section seeks to preserve the high

and fully recalled
also to set down for you along with my interpretations,
vouching for their truth;
3b. for not in those who have much to say did I delight,
as do the many
but in those who teach what is true,
nor in those who mention commandments derived from
other sources,

---

rhetorical color of the original (cf. Schwartz, *AkGWG*, 1904, 9-10). This warns us to handle the text with care; but it does not make impossible some discussion of what Papias was after.

Three typical solutions may be sketched here: (1) In sec. 4 the apostles listed are the "elders" referred to; hence "elders" in sec. 3a also refers to apostles; consequently, Papias claimed both direct acquaintance with apostles and also acquaintance with their immediate followers (Zahn, *Introduction*, II, 451-453; *Forschungen*, VI, 112-147). (2) Eusebius (3.39.5-7) already ignores sec. 3 in the discussion, apparently regarding sec. 4 as the heart of the matter; consequently, Papias claims only acquaintance with the immediate followers of the apostles. (3) "What Andrew," etc. ought to be translated "(as to) what Andrew," etc.—that is, the "elders" are the followers of the apostles listed. In that event Papias claimed only third-hand acquaintance, or, if sec. 3 is taken seriously, secondhand acquaintance at best. The correspondence between sec. 3a and sec. 4a, sec. 3b and sec. 4b, suggests that sec. 4 puts the case more precisely than sec. 3 (cf. Beyschlag, *TU*, LXXIX, 277). As to whether Papias has in mind the apostles when he says "elders," that seems to depend on factors external to the fragment. Thus sec. 7 seems to show that Papias' information was in fact derived primarily from Aristion and the elder John and that he was probably not even in direct contact with them; moreover, if one regards the traditions of the "elders" in Irenaeus as derived from Papias, then he probably spoke of the "elders" as "disciples of the apostles" (*Adv. haer.* 5.36.2). We are inclined, then, to the third solution mentioned above.

The syntax of the fragment is unclear. Eusebius may have taken *ha* in *ha te Aristiōn*, etc., to be a relative, thereby securing direct contact of Papias with Aristion and the elder John (since they "are saying"— to Papias presumably—the same things that Papias gathers from the followers of the presbyters). See *H.E.* 3.39.7 (where Eusebius is rightly doubtful of his deduction). C. Lambot (*Revue Bénédictine*, 43 [1931], 116-123) tries to make this solution more precise. He argues that *ha te Aristiōn kai ho presbyteros Iōannēs . . . legousi* is indeed in apposition to the preceding interrogative clauses (*ha*, the relative; *te . . . kai*, "both Aristion and John"). By taking into account the full context, this leaves Papias saying that he gained his information from

but in those who mention the commandments
given by the Lord to faith
and coming from the Truth itself.

4a. And if by chance someone should come who had actually attended the elders,
I examined the words of the elders,
what Andrew or what Peter said,

---

hearers of the presbyters and that "Aristion and John are precisely those presbyters whose listeners Papias was interrogating." But surely the order of the words would have to be *ha Aristiōn te kai ho presbyteros* to bear any such interpretation.

Tous tōn presbyterōn logous and *ha te Aristiōn*, etc. may be coordinate objects of *anekrinon* (this makes a sharp distinction between the apostles and the last two named individuals). But direct interrogative pronouns (*ti*) and relative pronouns (*ha*) are interchangeable (J. Munck, *HTR*, 52 [1959], 237, n. 41; cf. BAG, 558, 827), and the rhetorical structure points most naturally to this solution (cf. Schwartz, *AkGWG*, 1904, 10; he also suggests that the difference in tense between "said" and "were saying" reflects a striving for variety and does not necessarily imply that Aristion and the elder John were still alive; so also Lightfoot, *Essays*, 150, n. 3, who regards *legousi* as a historic present).

Nevertheless, some distinction between the apostles and the last two individuals named is implicit in the remark. What is the nature of that distinction? One typical solution is that of J. Chapman, *John the Presbyter* (Oxford, 1911), who thinks that it is a distinction between what could be gathered from apostles in past days (in Palestine) and what could be learned from Aristion and the elder John in a later time (in Asia). This makes it possible to regard the apostle John and the elder John as in fact one and the same. We are dealing with two generations and with an exceptional survivor from one to the other (see also J. F. Bligh, *ThS*, 13 [1952], 234-240). But "it would be unnatural to describe the same person in this way with an interval of barely more than a line" (J. Munck, *HTR*, 52 [1959], 238). I think we have to do with two Johns, though it is not quite certain that they are both of Asia; perhaps that should be assumed only of the elder (B. W. Bacon, *ZNW*, 12 [1911], 176-187, argues tenuously that even the elder was Palestinian).

Why, then, are the apostles called "disciples" when this title is shared also by Aristion and the elder John? And why is John and not Aristion called the elder? J. Munck (*HTR*, 52 [1959], 223-243) has shown that in our period (1) "elder" implies *antiquity and authority* (so Lightfoot) and could be applied to apostles and other ancient authorities, (2) that "disciples of the Lord" refers to (*a*) the Twelve, (*b*) "personal disciples of Jesus," (*c*) Christians in general (Acts

or what Philip,
or what Thomas or James,
or what John or Matthew,
or any other of the Lord's disciples,
and that which Aristion and the elder John,
    disciples of the Lord,
        were saying:

9:1), and (3) that sense (*b*) seems to apply in the case of Aristion and John the elder (they are distinguished from apostles yet are men of a particular qualification). Consequently (4) there could be other "elders" who were not necessarily "disciples"; hence (5) we see why our authorities are identified as they are—Papias wishes to assure us that in the case of Aristion and John the elder we are also dealing with eyewitnesses. (6) John is dubbed "the elder" (and not Aristion) probably to distinguish him from the apostle just mentioned (whether the term "elders" above embraces the apostles mentioned or not—Munck thinks it does); perhaps he simply held the office of "elder" in the church (Munck); yet in light of sec. 15 it seems more likely that "the elder" was a special designation for this man. Jerome (*De Viris Inlustribus* 18) thought that he was author of 2 and 3 John, who also identifies himself as "the elder"; but here again we have to contend with the apparent theological divergence between the world of the Gospel and epistles of John and the views of the elder(s).

It may be noted that some have suggested dropping the phrase "the Lord's disciples" in reference to Aristion and John as a dittography (Th. Mommsen, *ZNW*, 3 [1902], 156-159); many emendations have been suggested (see B. W. Bacon, *DCG*, I, 115-116), including especially "disciples of John" (W. Larfeld, *Byzantinisch-neugriechische Jahrbücher*, 3 [1922], 282-285), understood by E. Bammel (*RGG*, V [1961], 48) as referring to disciples of John the Baptist (cf. Acts 19:1-7). All this, we have seen, is unnecessary.

Is there a polemical intent in the prologue? (*a*) Many regard the prologue as anti-Gnostic. The talk about "the many" parallels that in Polycarp to the Philippians 2:1; *allotrias* implies heresy (cf. Ign. Trall. 6:1); the "many things" spoken by some may be long works like the *Exegetica* of Basilides (Clem. *Str.* 4.81.1); the concern for tradition may have been intended to counter Gnostic claims to secret—and oral—tradition (cf. Irenaeus, *Adv. haer.* 3.2.1; Tertullian, *De Praescriptione* 21: *viva voce*). None of this, however, is explicit; moreover, some of the elements may reflect simply rhetorical stock in trade: the attitude toward those "speaking many things" (Hecetaeus in Ps-Demetrius, *De Elecutione* 12, who also insists that what he has to say is "true" and introduces his statement about the "many words" of the Greeks with a "for"); the "living voice" (Quintilian, *Inst.* 2.2.7: *viva*

4b. for I assumed that what is derived from books does not
profit me
so much as what is derived from a living and abiding
voice."

5. Here it is worth noting that he twice enumerates the name John: the former of these he includes in the list with Peter and James and Matthew and the other apostles—clearly indicating that he has the Evangelist in mind; the other John he sets with others outside the number of the apostles by use of a distinguishing phrase placing Aristion before him; and he clearly calls him

---

vox as opposed to *lectio*; cf. Plato, *Phaedrus* 275d). (*b*) Others have suggested that Papias is unhappy about Paul and have noted the absence of anything Pauline in the fragments (also observe that "apostle"—avoided by Papias—is found primarily in Paul and Luke-Acts; "disciple" in Matthew, Mark, and John). (*c*) Others think Papias is rejecting John's Gospel, which refers often to Jesus' "commandments." The case for a polemical orientation is less strong in the decisive second half of the prologue. By "books" (literally "the books"; but I do not think that can be taken here as a reference to sacred writings as in 2 Clem. 14:2; the article is probably generic) it may be that Papias is thinking of written Christian commentary on Christ's teaching; some have thought that he had a document like the Gospel of John in mind. In any event, he does not seem *hostile* to these "books." (He may even mean his own written sources, such as Mark and Matthew.) I see no reason why all or most of what he says may not represent rhetorical flourishes and "conventional remarks" (Munck) having no more precise polemical intent than, say, the prologue to Luke's Gospel. If something else is involved, it may be no more than an echo of Jewish ideas of tradition: thus Philo, *De Vita Mosis* 1.4 derives information (*manthanein ek!*) on Moses both from the sacred "books" and from tradition mediated through "elders"!

Evidence for the use of the Gospel of John by Papias includes here the designation of Jesus as the Truth (John 14:6) and the order in which the apostles are named (John 1:40-43; 11:16).

We know nothing of Aristion. It is quite uncertain whether we can follow Conybeare and link him with the Aristo named in connection with the inauthentic ending of Mark in the Armenian Codex Etschmiadzin 229 (see B. W. Bacon, *DCG*, I, 116-118).

Finally, it should be noted that our prologue is incomplete and presupposes something said about written sources and their interpretation (to which oral tradition is "also" added). *Hermēneia* in the relevant sources means primarily (1) interpretation and (less often) (2) translation (H. J. Lawlor, *Hermathena*, 43 [1922], 170-171; for further discussion see on sec. 15). Only the former applies here. This

"elder." 6. Consequently, he demonstrates also in these remarks that their account is true who have said that two persons in Asia had the same name and that there were two graves in Ephesus, each of which even now is said to be John's [Eusebius, *H.E.* 7.25.16]. One must pay close attention to these things. For it is likely that the second—should one be unwilling to admit it of the first—saw the Revelation which is in circulation under the name of John. 7. And Papias, of whom we are now speaking, confesses that he received the words of the apostles from those who had attended them; but he says that he was himself a hearer of Aristion and the presbyter John. At all events, he often mentions them by name and sets forth their traditions in his writings. We may hope that what we have said here is of some use.

IIB. Extraordinary accounts (Eusebius, *H.E.* 3.39.8-10)

8. It is worth adding to the words of Papias that have been adduced other texts in which he relates some other extraordinary things as well as though they had reached him by tradition.

9. As to the fact that Philip the apostle had resided in Hierapolis along with his daughters, that was shown above [*H.E.* 3.31];

---

understanding of the passage fits in with what can be gathered about Papias' procedure from the first fragment. Presumably, then, the main burden of the five books was exposition of written *logia* (contained in Matthew and Mark, as secs. 15 and 16 show).

6. The reference here is to Dionysius' analysis of Revelation preserved by Eusebius (*H.E.* 7.25.16). The existence of two such tombs proves nothing. But the passage indicates that from the start Eusebius was intent on separating Revelation from the Gospel of John. He does not, however, press his claims too far; and the presence of a polemical perspective does not necessarily mean that Eusebius was wrong in seeing in Papias' prologue evidence for two Johns. But he took it too easily for granted that they were both of Ephesus.

7. The end of sec. 7 suggests that Eusebius deduced Papias' acquaintance with Aristion and the elder John from frequent references to them in his writing. There is, then, some doubt (such is the force of *goun;* cf. E. I. Robson, *JTS,* 14 [1913], 595) whether even this was anywhere explicitly stated or implied. In any event, both here and in sec. 14 it appears that Aristion and the elder John were, one way or the other, the real source of the oral tradition to which Papias appeals.

9. For these stories in Papias see also fragment XI (though it is not certain that this represents an independent witness). Eusebius

but that Papias, a contemporary of theirs, recalls having received a wonderful story from the daughters of Philip, must now be indicated: For he relates that the resurrection of a dead body took place in his day; furthermore, that another extraordinary event took place having to do with Justus who was surnamed Barsabas: he drank a deadly poison and through the Lord's grace suffered nothing unpleasant.

10. The books of Acts [1:17, 23, 24] relates that after the ascension of the Savior, the holy apostles set forth this Justus with

---

seems to have found it possible to interpret Papias as claiming direct contact only with the daughters of Philip (understand *chronous* with *kata tous autous* in line with the historian's usage elsewhere?); otherwise we might expect to find him embarrassed at uncovering evidence that Papias did after all know an "apostle." As to the identification of Philip and his daughters, I think it most likely that this is simply a confusion between Philip the "evangelist" (see Acts 21:8) and the "apostle" Philip. There is, to be sure, some suggestion of a separate tradition in Asia Minor about the "apostle" with three (or is it two?) daughters (*H.E.* 3.31.3; P. Corssen, *ZNW*, 2 [1901], 289-291; Lawlor-Oulton, II, 116-118), but the text may be corrupt (Schwartz, *AkGWG*, 1904, 16-17; see further, Zahn, *Forschungen*, VI, 158-175). Eusebius, however, and not Papias may be responsible for labeling Philip "apostle"; for in *H.E.* 3.31 the same identification is made by him (and his Asian source). (Perhaps we may also have expected the daughters of Philip to figure in the prologue had the apostle been intended.) It is not impossible that the evangelist and his daughters moved from Caesarea to Hierapolis; in considering the possibilities of contact with Papias, it must be remembered that ca. A.D. 58 the daughters of Philip were "virgins who prophesied"—presumably young women of some maturity; this does not rule out contact between them and Papias; yet it may be Eusebius who supplies the synchronisms in our text, whereas Papias may have been as vague here as he was in the prologue as to the directness of his contact with early authorities. The historical evaluation of our passage has become entangled with the problem of the relation between the "daughters of Philip" and "Quadratus"; they are linked twice in later tradition (*H.E.* 3.37.1; 5.17.3) and the latter also speaks of resurrections—if he is the Quadratus whose apology is quoted by Eusebius in *H.E.* 4.3.2 (cf. Zahn, *Forschungen*, VI, 41-53). Not much light is thrown on our passage by these tantalizing bits of information, however, as the complex and opposing arguments of Corssen (*ZNW*, 2 [1901], 289-299) and Chapman (*John the Presbyter*, 64-71) show.

For Justus Barsabas see Acts 1:23; and for the drinking of poison, Mark 16:18. The atmosphere is that of the later legendary acts (cf.

Matthias and prayed over the lot which was to determine how their number was to be filled out to make up for the traitor Judas; it runs somewhat as follows: "And they set forth two—Joseph called Barsabas who was surnamed Justus, and Matthias; and they prayed and said . . ."

IIC. The thousand years (Eusebius, H.E. 3.39.11-13)

11. And the same man has set out other things as coming to him from unwritten tradition—some strange parables of the Savior and teachings of his and some other mythical things.

12. Among them he mentions a certain period of a thousand years after the resurrection from the dead when Christ's kingdom will be established physically upon this earth of ours.

I rather suspect that he came up with these things through a misinterpretation of the apostolic accounts which he received, not comprehending what was said by them mystically and figuratively. 13. For he appears to be a man of very little intelligence, to judge from his writings; nevertheless, he was the reason that the great number of churchmen after him, on the grounds that he was a man of the primitive period, shared this opinion—I mean,

---

Acts of John 7-12). The complex arguments of Beyschlag (*TU*, LXXIX, 275-276) to prove that a specifically Gnostic motif lies in the background are unconvincing.

12. Once again it becomes clear that it is Papias' chiliasm that offends Eusebius (cf. 3.39.6, 13). He had in mind such things as are contained in fragment I. In this connection I do not see any evidence (*a*) that Eusebius was offended for any other reason (e.g., because Papias said nasty things about Luke or John or dated John's death too early; see below) or (*b*) that Papias' chiliasm is any more anti-Gnostic than that of his Jewish sources.

13. "A man of very little intelligence" may be a phrase from Papias' own work. If so, we may have something like their original setting in Victorinus, *De Fabr. Mund.* 9, where the author speaks of himself as a *mens parva*. In view of the fact that such self-evaluation was expected, the connection is not necessary (Hommes pp. 225-227); but it is not impossible. If the words do go back to Papias, Eusebius turned them against their author in an unwarranted way. (The conflicting evaluation of Papias by Eusebius in *H.E.* 3.36.2 may represent a later intrusion; Schwartz does not print it in his text.)

THE FRAGMENTS OF PAPIAS   105

for example, Irenaeus and all others who have expressed similar thoughts.

IID. Papias' sources (Eusebius, H.E. 3.39.14-17)

14. In his work he hands on as well other accounts of Aristion —to whom we alluded above—concerning the words of the Lord and other traditions of the presbyter John; although we refer those eager for knowledge to these, we feel constrained to add now to his words already presented a tradition concerning Mark the Gospel writer which he sets forth in these words:

14-17. Eusebius turns to the canon. Lightfoot (*Essays*, 32-58) has shown by combining Eusebius' formal remarks in *H.E.* 3.3.3-7; 3.25.1-7 and his actual practice (*a*) that Eusebius makes mention of accepted books (the four Gospels, Acts, thirteen epistles of Paul) only when the writer "has something to *tell about them*," (*b*) that he notes the use of books ("testimonies") which are not agreed upon (Hebrews, Revelation), (*c*) that the catholic epistles are on the borderline but that in practice "testimonies" of 1 John and 1 Peter are noted, (*d*) that what is said or used of noncanonical books of some authority—such as the Gospel According to the Hebrews—is noted.

Silence about Paul, Luke, and John, then, needs not indicate that Papias did not know these writings. There is some evidence that he used John (see pp. 101, 130). Some regard Papias' words on Mark as having affinities with the prologue of Luke (*anataxasthai, parakoloutheti, akribōs, kathexēs*), but in that event it is hard to decide whether Luke is reacting to Papias (Annand, *SJT*, 9 [1956], 50-51) or Papias to Luke (R. M. Grant, *ATR*, 25 [1943], 219). In the latter case he may be using Luke as a standard or hinting that his own work is superior. It does seem that Papias represents a *non-Pauline* type of Christianity (and that may have something to do with his lack of interest in Luke—a follower of Paul by early accounts). There is no evidence that Papias was *anti-Pauline*, though he may have regarded the apostle as insufficiently concerned about the things that really matter—the "oracles of the Lord."

Bauer (*Rechtgläubigkeit*, 187, 189) suggests that Eusebius did not report what Papias said about Luke and John because Papias regarded them with suspicion; in the case of Luke (and Paul) he was overreacting to Marcion! Schwartz thinks (see p. 118) that Eusebius was dissatisfied with Papias' early dating of John's death. The evidence for these views is very tenuous.

Another point must be kept in mind: Eusebius may have been dependent on selections from Papias' work. B. Gustafsson (*TU*, LXXIX, 431-433) has shown that Eusebius' "fairly rigid habit" is to

106   THE APOSTOLIC FATHERS

15. (a) "And the elder used to say this:
　　Mark, having been Peter's translator,
　　　wrote all that he remembered
　　　　accurately
　　　　but not in order
　　　　as to what was either said or done by the Lord;

give precise reference to particular books in a work whenever possible. He does not do so here. This may explain his silence on some points.

Finally, it is possible that Papias wrote before the appearance of one or more of the books in question—Luke or John (or even Matthew if sec. 16 is understood to refer to something other than the Gospel; cf. Annand, *SJT*, 9 [1956], 57). But I think this unlikely.

15. Once again the rhetorical balance of the lines is to be noted. The style is the same as the prologue. This means that Papias has reworked whatever he received from "the elder" (John?). It is impossible, then, to distinguish between Papias and his source at this point.

There is also a good chance that some technical rhetorical language is used here by Papias in his analysis of Mark. *Order:* (*a*) F. H. Colson, *JTS*, 14 [1913], 67-69 has shown that *taxis* is a technical rhetorical term, that it was also applied to historical writing (cf. Lucian, *Quomodo Historia Conscribenda Sit* 48; Dionysius, *Iudicium De Thycidide* 10-20), and that consequently Papias was possibly speaking not of chronological but of literary order. Colson judges that absence of "order" in the case of Mark would have to do with the abrupt beginning, the incomplete ending, the admission of "trivial" points; possibly also the absence of set speeches and the inferior grouping of materials. (*b*) A. Wright, *JTS*, 14 (1913), 298-300, holds against Colson that the criticism of Mark has to do with defective knowledge; and he defends the view that the chronology of the Fourth Gospel is the standard whereby Papias was judging Mark (cf. Lightfoot, *Essays*, 205–209). (*c*) Others point out that the second part of the statement—presumably again the most informative part ("so that")—has to do with the *incompleteness*, not the *order*, of Mark. In this connection, T. Mullins, *VC*, 14 (1960), 216–220, shows that *enia* ("some") often implies "a few." To give unity to our text, J. A. Kleist (*Saint Louis University Studies: Series A, Humanities*, Vol. I, No. 1 [St. Louis, 1945], 13-15) renders *taxei* "in full detail." I find the linguistic arguments in favor of this weak. I would like to suggest that defective literary order in itself would imply the possibility of omissions; thus Quintilian (*Inst.* 7. Praef. 3) asserts that the rhetorician would "repeat many things, omit many things" if his "order" were inadequate.

Chria: I have adopted the suggestion of R. O. P. Taylor, *The*

(b) for he neither heard the Lord
nor attended him,
but later, as I said, (he attended) Peter,
who presented his teachings in *chria*-form
but not with the aim of constructing an ordered
arrangement of the dominical oracles;

Groundwork of the Gospels (Oxford, 1946), 75-90, that this does not mean "with a view to whatever needs (*chriai*) arose," but has to do with a literary form discussed by the rhetoricians. The *chria* was "a concise and pointed *account* of something *said or done*, attributed to some particular person" (Theon; ed. Walz, I, 201). Quintilian (*Inst.* 1.9.5) regarded a *chria* based on the acts of people as unusual. As modern "form criticism" recognizes, the term has some relevance to what was "said and done" by Jesus. The *chria* played a role particularly in the *preliminary* training of the orator—hence the inadequacy of Mark's account which reflected the undeveloped literary procedures of Peter.

Recollected: This verb plays a role in close connection with the *chria*: "Why is the *chria* a recollection (*apomnēmoneuma*)? Because it is recollected (*apomnēmoneuetai*) in order that it may be quoted" (from a third-century papyrus). A less technical sense, of course, is clearly possible (cf. Eusebius, *H.E.* 5.20.6).

Translator: I have left this term (found at the beginning of sec. 15) to the end because I do not think a rhetorical background is implied. *Hermēneutēs* means primarily (a) interpreter or (b) translator. The former seems unlikely. Papias is concerned about his sources here, not about "interpretations" or "expositions" (as in sec. 3); a point is even made of the fact that Mark stuck close—too close!—to Peter's very words. I think that Papias is speaking of translation. J. Kürzinger (*BZ*, 4 [1960], 25-28), however, derives its meaning from the rhetorical use of *hermēneia* and *hermēneuō*. He claims that these terms deal basically with "mediation," and that consequently Mark became Peter's *hermēneutēs* ("Mittelsmann") by the very act of setting forth Peter's gospel (cf. Zahn, *Introduction*, II, 454-456). It is correct that these words have to do with "mediation"; but in all the examples I have met in the rhetorical handbooks they refer to the movement within a man by which his thoughts become words; hence the normal significance of *hermēneia* is "style" and of *hermēneuō* "to express" something. Consequently the verb regularly occurs in these sources with an adverb indicating the kind of style; and a noun *hermēneutēs* in the proposed sense does not exist.

That Mark is called "translator" possibly presupposes a Jewish model. For it was normal practice to provide a *methurgaman* for (a) the readings from the Hebrew Bible and (b) the homilies of the preachers (P. Gächter, *Zeitschrift für katholische Theologie*, 60

(a) so that Mark did nothing wrong
when he wrote some down as he recollected them;
(b) for he concerned himself for one thing—

[1936], 161-187). Strikingly enough, although the formula "to omit nothing . . . nor to introduce any falsehood" (or something like this) occurs in Hellenistic as well as biblical and Jewish sources (W. C. van Unnik, *VC*, 3 [1949], 1-36; *ZNW*, 54 [1963], 276-277), it is also applied specifically to the activity of the *methurgaman* who translates homilies (Tosephta Megilla 4.41). (For the view that Mark was translator of Peter's *written* testimony, that he added "some [few] things" which he remembered, and that Papias is defending him against the charge of altering apostolic writing, see T. Mullins, *VC*, 14 [1960], 220-224. This requires an unnatural shift of attention from written to oral sources in the first line of the fragment.) The Basilidians regarded Glaukias as Peter's *hermēneus* (Clement, *Str.* 7.106); apparently they too thought that the apostle spoke Aramaic.

There is a slight possibility that the figure of Socrates also plays a role in this passage. Mark's "recollecting" may have reminded Papias as it did Justin later (*Apol.* 1.66.3, 67.3) of the *Memorabilia* (*apomnēmoneumata*) of Xenophon. Note also that the words *ta lechthenta kai prachthenta* occur in Plato's *Phaedo* 58c, where they have to do with a request for full details about Socrates' death.

Papias' remarks on Mark need not represent a reaction to criticism of the Gospel from other quarters. They may well arise from Papias' own "literary criticism" and a desire to establish the reliability of his sources (cf. secs. 3-4). He refers to the incompleteness of Mark primarily because he is interested in the "oracles of the Lord" and Mark does not provide him with all that he wants. What Mark lacks, Matthew has (sec. 16). Papias probably had in mind the fuller beginning and end of Matthew but especially, I think, the great collections of words of Jesus in the first gospel. The term *logia*, to be sure, embraces both "things said and done" by Jesus, but the emphasis is on things said (cf. Justin, *Dial.* 17-18; Irenaeus *Adv. haer.* 1.8). It is precisely such oracles of the Lord that formed the subject of Papias' book (sec. 1). It seems to me likely, then, that *enia* does not mean "some things" but "some (oracles)" and that the relatively few number of them in Mark is being measured against the larger number supplied by Matthew. Thus lack of *taxis* in Mark involves primarily lack of a *syntaxis* (orderly arrangement, composition) of the oracles of the Lord; and that clearly implies incompleteness in this respect. I judge it unlikely, then, that either Luke or John formed the standard by which Mark is judged. I cannot here summarize all that goes to support this view elsewhere in our analysis of the fragments, especially since the evidence is tenuous; but I do think a somewhat stronger case can be

to omit nothing of what he heard
nor to introduce any falsehood in them."
Such, then, is Papias' account concerning Mark.

16. Concerning Matthew he says this: "Now Matthew made an

---

made for taking sayings of the Marcan-Matthaean type as the main point of departure for Papias' "interpretations."

Zahn (*Introduction*, II, 449-450; cf. Schwartz, AkGWG, 1904, 18-20) thought that Eusebius, *H.E.* 2.15 cast further light on Papias' treatment of Mark (Mark and Peter linked also with the help of 1 Pet. 5:13 [cf. *H.E.* 6.25.5-6]); but this is unlikely (A. von Harnack, ZNW, 3 [1902], 159-166; P. Corssen, ZNW, 3 [1902], 244-245). Clement (*H.E.* 6.14.6-7) and Origen (*H.E.* 6.25.5) tell us that Peter was still alive when Mark wrote the Gospel. But it seems more likely that *genomenos* in Papias presupposes Peter's death (Lawlor-Oulton, II, 115-116).

16. After all that has been said of the *logia* above, there is hardly any doubt that Papias had in mind here the Gospel of Matthew —not a collection of OT oracles (R. Harris) or a collection of sayings of Jesus like "Q" (Schleiermacher). We may note that evidence for a testimony book behind Matthew is very weak; see J. A. Findley in *Amicitiae Corolla* (London, 1933), 57-71.

We again render *hermēneuō* "translate." It could mean "expound"; but it seems to me that the reference to Matthew's Hebrew original makes this the unlikely choice. Some argue that if Papias had been concerned about translation, he would have said something as to how an authoritative Greek version of Matthew had come into being. But how can we know that? The problem never seems to have troubled others in the early Church (cf. Eusebius, *H.E.* 3.24.6; 5.10.3; 6.25.4; Irenaeus, *Adv. haer.* 3.1.2). Moreover, it is possible that once again a Jewish model is involved: the *methurgaman* turned Matthew into Greek orally as it was read before the assembled church (R. O. P. Taylor). It is likely, then, that Papias did not have in mind anything to do with the *written* translation of Matthew.

Such activity, however, lay in the past, as the tense of the verb shows. Papias is working with a Greek Matthew. Whether there ever was a Hebrew Matthew is another question which the majority of modern scholars answer in the negative. (For a defense of the theory see D. A. Frövig, *Neue kirchliche Zeitschrift*, 42 [1931], 344-376.) Why does Papias advance the theory (or bring forward this fact)? It is possible (Lightfoot, *Essays*, 208-209) that he was trying to explain away contradictions between Matthew and another Gospel (though this does not necessarily imply that he was responding to Gnostic criticism of the Church's Gospel). I incline to think, however, that he was simply underscoring the reliability of his (major?) written sources

ordered arrangement of the oracles in the Hebrew language, and each man translated them as he was able."

17. The same author made use of testimonies from the first letter of John and likewise from that of Peter; and he set forth also another account concerned with a woman reproached for many sins in the Lord's presence [cf. John 7:53–8:11], which the Gospel According to the Hebrews contains. So much for these things which we have felt constrained to note in addition to what has been set forth already.

---

by showing that they were based one way or the other on the language actually spoken by Jesus. Disciples of Jesus—Matthew as well as Peter—could be expected to use the "Hebrew language" (Aramaic?). Unlike Peter, who contented himself with occasional utterances, Matthew put together the *logia* in a systematic and (to Papias) more satisfying way. The notice on Matthew, then, is not necessarily derogatory. (It is even possible to take *oun* in a somewhat adversative sense [BAG, 597] and to assume that these words followed immediately on the remarks about Mark. Otherwise *oun* presupposes a fuller preceding discussion of Matthew.)

J. Kürzinger (*Biblische Zeitschrift*, 4 [1960], 32-35; *New Testament Studies*, 10 [1963], 109-115) understands the passage differently: Matthew composed the *logia* in a Hebraic style; thus each man—Mark and Matthew—set them forth (*hermēneusen*) as he was able. We have already shown Kürzinger's interpretation of *hermēneuō* and *hermēneutēs* to be wrong. As for *dialektos*, it is true that the rhetoricians use it to mean "style." But the adjectives that go with it are terms like "exalted," "poetic," "one's own," etc. To be sure, Dionysius refers to the "Platonic style" (*Ad Pompeium* 2 [758]); but even that, I think, is of another order. Moreover, there is no significance in the fact that Papias unlike Acts (1:19; 21:40; 22:2; 26:14) does not use the definite article in this connection (see the examples of *dialektos* and *glōssa* with proper adjectives in the passages referred to by Leisegang in his index to Philo, pp. 165, 178).

17. The story of the woman probably is that now contained in many MSS of John 7:53–8:11. The evidence for a specifically Papian form of the narrative preserved either in the Armenian Codex Etschmiadzin 229 (cf. B. W. Bacon, *Expositor*, 6/11 [1905], 161-177) or by Agapius (J. Linder, *Zeitschrift für katholische Theologie* 40 [1916], 191-199) is weak (U. Becker, *Jesus und die Ehebrecherin* [Berlin, 1963], 92-116). The reference to "many sins" (rather than adultery) may indicate that we are dealing with a different story entirely. In any event, it is Eusebius who links it with the Gospel According to the Hebrews. Naturally this does not exclude the possibility that Papias derived the story from that source.

III. Judas (Apollinaris of Laodicaea; the text, preserved in commentaries and catenae, follows the reconstruction of E. Preuschen, *Antilegomena* [Giessen, 1905], 97-99)

1. From Apollinarius: Judas did not die by hanging but was taken down before he was strangled and lived on. This the Acts of the Apostles shows: "falling headlong he burst open in the middle, and his bowels gushed out" [Acts 1:18]. This fact Papias the disciple of John relates more clearly in the fourth book of the Exposition of the Dominical Oracles as follows:

2. "Judas walked about in this world a great example of impiety, his flesh so swollen that he found it impossible to pass through a place where a wagon easily passes; indeed this was true of the mass of his head alone. For his eyelids, they say, were so swollen up that he did not see light at all, and his eyes could not

---

The account is handed on from (1) Apollinarius (Latin form: Apollinaris) of Laodicaea (*ca.* A.D. 310–390) or, less likely, (2) Apollinarius, bishop of Hierapolis, the city of Papias (last half of the second century). The former wrote many commentaries (now lost); the latter did not (cf. Eusebius, *H.E.* 4.27.1; 5.16.1; 5.19.2). For other reasons favoring the selection of the Laodicaean see Zahn, *Forschungen*, VI, 126, n. 1. Our Apollinarius was seeking to harmonize Matthew 27:3-10 with Acts 1:16-20 (see also Augustine, *Contra Felicem* 1.4 and the Vulgate). The attempt at suicide (Matthew) was unsuccessful; Judas lived on and met a terrible end (Acts). The translation "swelling up" instead of "falling headlong" in Acts 1:18 seems to be based on authorities who have pushed harmonizing tendencies even further by drawing together Acts and Papias more closely; the rendering is scarcely defensible (K. Lake in *Beginnings of Christianity*, V [London, 1933], 27-29).

One form of the text (*Catena in Evangelium S. Matthaeum*, ed. Cramer [Oxford, 1840], 231) has Judas killed by the wagon whose size he rivals and there it ends; all the following details are attributed to Apollinarius. This may be correct. Independent (?) witness, however, from Bar Salibi definitely connects the passage about the worms with Papias.

This account of Judas comes from the same fourth book of Papias as did our first fragment. Both seem to use passages not far distant from one another in Matthew as points of departure. Just how Papias related Matthew 27:3-10 to his story about Judas is not clear; but it seems overbold to assume that Matthew did not yet contain the account (Bartlet in *Amicitiae Corolla*, 37-38).

The Judas pericopes in John, Mark, and Acts reflect psalms (John 13:8 and Mark 14:18/Ps. 41:9; Acts 1:16-20/Pss. 69:25 and 109:8)

be detected even with the help of a physician's optical instrument; that is how deep they were imbedded below the surface. His genitals appeared more loathesome and larger than the private parts of any other; and even when he relieved himself, there passed through them, to his shame, pus and worms which flowed together from every part of his body. 3. After many agonies and punishments, they say, he died in his own place, which to the present day is desolate and uninhabited from the ill odor; nor can anyone to this day pass that spot without holding his nose. Even on the ground the flow which spread from his flesh was so great!"

---

and seem to presuppose a wide application to Judas of passages about the "enemy" (K. Lüthi, *Evangelische Theologie*, 16 [1956], 102-103; B. Gärtner, *Svensk Exegetisk Årsbok*, 21 [1956], 56-61). It is possible, then, that Papias' account of Judas' swelling and hindered vision is to be connected with Ps. 109:18 (cf. Num. 5:21, 22, 27) and Ps. 69:23 (E. Schweizer, *ThZ*, 14 [1958], 46). Papias, then, would be drawing on a pre-Lucan tradition which interpreted the figure of Judas basically in terms of the fulfillment of prophecy. (For the OT background to the NT passages about Judas see P. Benoit in *Synoptische Studien*, Festschrift Alfred Wikenhauser [Munich, 1953], 1-19.)

At the same time, the grotesque details of the story also receive inspiration from more or less standard themes in the accounts of the death of wicked men: 2 Maccabees 9:7-12; Josephus, *Ant*. 17.169, and *Bell*. 7.453; Ahikar (in R. H. Charles, *Apocrypha and Pseudepigrapha* [Oxford, 1913], II, 776); Acts 12:23, Tertullian, *Ad Scapulam* 3; Eusebius, *H.E.* 8.16.4-5. J. Herber was shown (*Revue de l'histoire des religions*, 129/30 [1945], 47-56) that the swelling and bursting of the belly is regarded in many religious traditions as a sign of visitation by demonic powers; he feels constrained, therefore, to link Papias' account of Judas with John 13:25-27.

It seems unlikely that a Gnostic dimension lies behind the text (Beyschlag, *TU*, LXXIX, 271-273). In particular, the dragon of the Acts of Thomas 32-33 who inspires Judas' betrayal and who himself swells and bursts may be modeled on Judas rather than the other way around; in any event, the text is from the third century. Gruesome accounts like that of Papias may indeed presuppose mythological archetypes, but they need not be those of a specifically Gnostic variety. Thus Lüthi believes the old "chaos" mythology, presumably connected with the figure of the "enemy" in the Psalms, lives on in the figure of Judas; already in John, Judas is virtually the Antichrist.

It is faintly possible that Papias' interpretation was intended to counter the positive evaluation of Judas in early Gnostic systems (Irenaeus, *Adv. haer.* 1.3.1; Tertullian, *Adversus Marcionem* 4.40).

IV. The fall of Satan (Andrew of Caesarea, *In Apocalypsim* cap. 34, serm. 12; *PG*, CVI, 325)

Here are the exact words of Papias: "He assigned some of them"—obviously he means some of those angels who were once divine—"to preside over the regulation of the earth and commanded them to rule well." Next he says: "Their administration came to no good end."

VI. The trustworthiness of Revelation (Andrew of Caesarea, *In Apocalypsim* Praef.; *PG*, CVI, 220)

Concerning the divine inspiration of the book [the Revelation of John] we think it superfluous to drag out the discussion, since the blessed Gregory—Gregory the theologian, I mean—and the blessed Cyril and those of an older generation as well—Papias,

---

Andrew (bishop of Caesarea in Cappadocia; *ca.* A.D. 563–614) is interpreting Revelation 12:7-8, which he understands (in part) of the casting out of Satan "because of pride and envy" after the creation of the world; Satan, he adds, had previously been entrusted with—and presumably retained—"authority in the air as the Apostle says" (cf. Eph. 2:2). The quotation from Papias is intended to support these views.

That (inferior classes of) angels were set over the various elements of nature at the time of creation (cf. Jub. 2:2) and that angels fell away from God (cf. Gen. 6:1-4; Jub. 4:22; 5:1-9; 1 Enoch 6:1 ff.) are Jewish teachings (G. F. Moore, *Judaism* [Cambridge, Mass., 1932], I, 403-404, 406). A close connection between the two themes is presupposed in Jude 6 and worked out in detail by the later Fathers of the Church (e.g., Athenagoras, *Leg.* 24–27; J. Daniélou, *Les anges et leur mission* [Éditions de Chevetogne, 1951], 62-67).

Papias' comment may have been made in connection with Matthew 25:41, which breathes something of the same atmosphere as Jude 6 and Revelation 12:7-8.

This passage forms an independent section in Andrew's preface. Neglected by Andrew here is Justin (*Dial.* 81), who represents another early witness to Revelation; he regards it as an apostolic writing and is enthusiastic about its millennial doctrine. Eusebius does not seem to know about Papias' use of Revelation or his attitude toward it (*H.E.* 3.39.14-17); this is all the more striking in view of his concern for the book in the same context (*H.E.* 3.39.6; cf. 7.25.1-27). Moreover, the use of "testimonies" from Revelation is one of the things which Eusebius comments on regularly (cf. *H.E.* 3.24.18; 3.25.2; 4.18.8; 4.24; 5.18.14; Lightfoot, *Essays*, 39, 47). (*a*) Does this mean that Eusebius

Irenaeus, Methodius, and Hippolytus—bear witness to its trustworthiness.

VI. The six days (Anastasius of Sinai, In Hexaëmeron I; J. B. Pitra, Analecta Sacra, II [1884], 160; cf. PG, LXXXIX, 860)

Taking our cue from the excellent Papias of Hierapolis, who was a disciple of the Bosom-Friend, and from Clement and Pantaenus, the priest of the Alexandrians, and from the most

---

had not fully examined Papias' work or that he knew it only through selections? (b) On the other hand, what evidence other than our fragment is there that Papias in fact used Revelation (though see p. 129)? Is it possible that Andrew made an unjustified inference? (c) Another point needs to be kept in mind: If Papias really thought that John the apostle was martyred ca. A.D. 44 (see p. 118), and if he ascribed Revelation (and the Gospel) to this John, then he must have dated Revelation (and the Gospel) in the Claudian reign (A.D. 41-54). Traces of such a dating are preserved especially in Epiphanius' account of the Alogi (Haereses 51.33). If this may be regarded as ultimately dependent on Papias, Eusebius' silence can be explained as an unwillingness to pass on what would seem to him absurdities concerning the Johannine corpus (Schwartz, AkGWG, 1904, 29-47). Epiphanius' date, however, may be the result of relatively late chronological blunders (cf. J. Chapman, JTS, 8 [1907], 603). Either way the arguments are complex and tenuous; in any event, there seems no way of demonstrating a necessary connection between Papias and these later speculations. Nor can we be sure that Eusebius would have suppressed such information.

The "theologian" was a title applied to Gregory of Nazianzus (Lampe p. 628). By Cyril is meant Cyril of Alexandria, since Cyril of Jerusalem excluded Revelation from his canon (Catecheses 4.36).

Anastasius (ca. A.D. 700) states that he undertakes the difficult task of setting forth an interpretation of the six days of creation conscious of his dependence (a) on Paul's teaching (in Hebrews; cf. PG, LXXXIX, 969) that what is in the law was written "as a type of Christ and his Church" and (b) the procedures of earlier commentators. By Clement he means, of course, Clement of Alexandria; by Pantaenus, Clement's teacher (Eusebius, H.E. 5.10.1-11.2; 6.14.8-9); by Ammonius, the contemporary of Origen who wrote a book on The Harmony of Moses and Jesus (H.E. 6.19.10). The "Bosom-Friend" (epistēthios) is a standard epithet for John the Evangelist in the Greek Fathers (P. A. Vacarri, Biblica, 20 [1939], 413-414). The MSS wrongly read en before tō epistēthiō phoitēsantos (its omission is supported by the next fragment in which Anastasius refers to Papias as a phoitētēs of John the Evangelist). Some MS evidence suggests that instead of "before the time of the councils" (pro tōn synodōn) we ought to read "all ancient and primitive (prōtōn) interpreters who

learned Ammonius—all men of the primitive period and interpreters before the time of the councils who understood the whole six days to refer to Christ and the Church.

VII. Paradise (Anastasius of Sinai, *In Hexaëmeron* VII; PG, LXXXIX, 961-962)

The ecclesiastical interpreters from very primitive times—I mean Philo, the philosopher, and contemporary of the apostles, and the famous Papias, the disciple of John the Evangelist, Irenaeus of Lyons and Justin the martyr and philosopher, Pantaenus the Alexandrian and Clement Stromateus, and their associates—understood the things about paradise spiritually and

---

agree with each other (*synōdōn*)." Cf. Zahn, *Forschungen*, VI, 126, n. 3.

Papias' interest in the six days is probably an aspect of his apocalyptic orientation; for the apocalyptic tradition was profoundly interpenetrated by the idea that the end would be as the beginning (cf. Barn. 6:13) and delighted in working out the parallels. It is possible that his interpretation is in large measure retained for us in Victorinus' fragmentary *De Fabricia Mundi* (ed. J. Haussleiter; cf. J. Chapman, *JTS*, 9 [1908], 49-52). Victorinus' exegesis of the days of creation may fairly be described as having to do with Christ and the Church; there are many references to the Apocalypse in the document; and where the Gospels are referred to, Matthew (perhaps the main point of departure for Papias) usually provides what our author wants (in particular Matt. 12:8, 19:8; 12:3-5, which in *De Fabr. Mund.* 5-6 are taken to point to the millennial significance of the Sabbath); see further, p. 129.

Elsewhere Anastasius is vividly conscious of the gulf that separates the Jewish philosopher Philo from Christianity (*Viae Dux* 14; *PG*, LXXXIX, 244-245); but he does not hesitate to refer to him as a man with a sound (allegorical) sense for scriptural interpretation (cf. *In Hexaem.* 7; *PG*, LXXXIX, 956). Clement is often called "Stromateus" by the later Fathers as writer of the *Stromata*. The two Gregorys are Gregory of Nazianzus and Gregory of Nyssa.

Anastasius believes (against Origen) that the "paradise" of Genesis had to do also with an earthly place but combats an excessively literal exposition of the details (*PG*, LXXXIX, 968-970). He employs exegetical traditions which favor a distinction between the "material" and "spiritual" or "terrestrial" and "celestial" paradise (*PG*, LXXXIX, 964-966). In some quarters it is likely that only the latter (more Jewish) contrast was relevant (cf. 2 Enoch 8:1-8). It is further possible that Papias accepted the existence of a celestial paradise

referred them to the Church of Christ. Of these are also the two Cappadocian Gregorys, who are profoundly learned in everything. All these . . . assert that there is also a certain spiritual paradise.

VII. "Children" (Maximus the Confessor, *Scholia in Dionysii Areopagitae De Caelesti Hierarchia* 2.5; *PG*, IV, 48)

They used to call those who practiced godly guilelessness "children," as also Papias shows in the first book of his *Dominical Expositions* and Clement of Alexandria in the *Pedagogue*.

---

alone, as in Irenaeus, *Adv. haer.* 5.5.1 and 5.36.1 (see below)—words attributed to the "elders" (cf. 1 Enoch 60:8; 61:12; 2 Cor. 12:4). Note that Anastasius' authorities quote Ezekiel 28:12-18 in this context and that a fragment of the same passage seems to appear in *Adv. haer.* 5.36.1 (Lightfoot, *Essays*, 199-201). Our guess is that the exegesis of the six days (Gen. 1:1-2:3; see fragment VI) had to do with creation and figuratively with Christ, the Church (the six days), and the millennium (the seventh day), whereas the story of Adam and the garden (Gen. 2:4-3:24) was taken to refer especially to the celestial paradise and man's fall from it.

Maximus is explaining how it is that (Ps-)Dionysius could address Timothy as "child" (*pais*). He offers three possible solutions, of which this is the last. Clement's definition of a "child" is lengthy and makes reference to many biblical passages in which terms like *pais*, *paidion*, *teknon*, and *nēpion* occur (*Paed.* 1.12.1-52.3). It is impossible, however, to find any one passage on which he hangs the discussion. Yet we may note that Irenaeus (*Adv. haer.* 4.41.2-3) also knows of a tradition from "one before (him)" which discusses the meaning of the term "son"; and just as Clement curiously refers in this connection to the gentle creatures symbolic of Christian "children" in Scripture (*Paed.* 1.14.1-15.4). so Irenaeus refers to less admirable creatures symbolic of sinners in Scripture (*Adv. haer.* 4.41.3). Interestingly enough, Irenaeus' first example is the "serpent" and Clement concludes his remarks on the subject by stating that "we children no longer roll about on the ground or creep forward on the earth like serpents . . ." (*Paed.* 1.16.3). Irenaeus quotes Matthew 23:33 ("generation of vipers") here and follows it by a reference to Matthew 16:6—a warning against Pharisees and Sadducees ("wicked and adulterous generation" in Matt. 16:4). "Generation of vipers" occurs also in the mouth of John the Baptist in Matthew 3:7, and there it also refers to Pharisees and Sadducees. Within a few verses (3:9) we are also told that God can raise up "children" (*tekna*) to Abraham from "these stones." Is this the setting of Papias' remarks?

IX. Enjoyment of food in the resurrection (Maximus the Confessor, *Scholia in Dionysii Areopagitae De Ecclesiastica Hierarchia* 7.2; *PG*, IV, 176)

He says this, I think, hinting at Papias, who was then bishop of Hierapolis in Asia and flourished at the same time as the divine evangelist John. For in his fourth book of the *Expositions of the Dominical Oracles* this Papias mentioned the enjoyment of food in the resurrection. Afterwards Apollinarius gave credence to this doctrine which some call the millennium. How then could the writings of the holy Dionysius [cf. Eusebius, *H.E.* 7.25] have been written by Apollinarius—as some foolishly maintain—since they refute Apollinarius? And Irenaeus of Lyons says the same thing in the fifth treatise of his book against the heresies and brings in the above-mentioned Papias as a witness to his statements.

X. Enjoyment of certain material food (Stephen Gobarus, summarized by Photius, *Bibliothecae Codices* 232; *PG*, CIII, 1104)

Nor again [does Stephen accept] either Papias, bishop of Hierapolis and martyr, or Irenaeus, the holy bishop of Lyons, where they say that the kingdom of heaven is the enjoyment of certain material food.

XI. An epitome of Papias' work (Philip of Side; C. de Boor, *Texte und Untersuchungen*, V [1888], 170)

1. Papias, bishop of Hierapolis, having been a hearer of John

---

Pseudo-Dionysius catalogues errors concerning the dead, of which one is that the lot promised the saints is like life in this world and that "food suitable to another way of life (is ascribed) wrongly to those who have become like angels." We have already met Apollinarius of Laodicaea (p. 111) and Dionysius of Alexandria (p. 102). For Irenaeus' teaching on the millennium see *Adv. haer.* 5.33.3-4 (fragment I) which is also connected with Papias.

Stephen (sixth century), according to Photius, dealt with special problems in eighteen chapters near the end of his theological treatise; this censure of Papias and Irenaeus was included there. Stephen may have been dependent on Irenaeus for his knowledge of Papias. For the language of our passage compare Romans 14:17. For the probable origin of the idea of Papias' martyrdom see p. 92.

The famous line on James and John is, in the words of Dix (*Theol-*

the theologian and companion of Polycarp, wrote five treatises on the *Dominical Oracles*. In them he made an enumeration of apostles, and after naming Peter and John, Philip and Thomas and Matthew, recorded as "disciples of the Lord" Aristion and another John whom he also called "elder." Consequently, some believe that this John was the author of the two short catholic epistles which are in circulation under the name of John, on the ground that the men of the primitive period accepted only the

---

ogy, 24 [1932], 19), "an isolated fragment of what may be an eighth-century epitome of what may be a reference by the lost fifth-century *History* of Philip of Side to something in Papias." The editor of our passage, de Boor, thought it probable that the epitomizer drew from Philip of Side (*TU*, V, 171-174). It seems clear that the first section is a summary (by the epitomizer or his source) of Eusebius, *H.E.* 3.39 with a few critical remarks added. (Jerome, *De Viris Inlustribus* 18—on Papias—also mentions the theory that 2 and 3 John were written by the elder rather than the apostle.) It is the second section which seems to draw in fresh material. For Eusebius either does not know or suppresses what Papias had to say about James and John; and the epitome's account of the two miracles goes beyond *H.E.* 3.39.9 in details.

The notice on the death of James and John has been correlated with other fragmentary information to uncover a tradition concerning the early death of John and thereby to discredit Irenaeus' remarks (*Adv. haer.* 2.22.5) about that apostle and the early Church's theories about the authorship of the Johannine corpus (Schwartz, A*k*GWG, 1904, No. 5; cf. *ZNW*, 15 [1914], 210-219): Mark 10:35-40 is a *vaticinium ex eventu* linking the death of James and John. Acts 12:2 makes it clear that the former was slain by the Jews in A.D. 44. Evidence of an early dating of Revelation is added (see p. 114). Revelation and the Gospel of John, then, were regarded by Papias as early authorities (consequently in *H.E.* 3.39.15-16 John is the standard whereby Mark and Matthew are judged). Eusebius did not report all this because it flew in the face of the current traditions about John and his writings.

On the other hand, however, Mark 10:35-40 may not refer to martyrdom (F. Spitta, *ZNW*, 11 [1910], 39-58; cf. E. Schwartz, *ZNW*, 11 [1910], 89-104; J. Weiss, *ZNW*, 11 [1910], 167). In any event, it is more likely to have given rise to the idea that John suffered martyrdom (and not necessarily *together* with James) than to be a reflection of this otherwise unknown fact (to claim that Acts 12:2 originally contained also the name of John is clearly arbitrary). The de Boor fragment, moreover, does not inspire confidence. John is called "the theologian" in fourth-century sources for the first time (Lampe p. 628). That the brothers were "slain by the Jews" is

first epistle. Some have also been misled into thinking that he was the author of Revelation. Now Papias is also wrong about the millennium, and from him Irenaeus derived the same error [cf. Eusebius, H.E. 3.39 (and 3.25)].

2. Papias in the second treatise says that John the theologian and James his brother were slain by the Jews. The aforesaid Papias related on the authority of the daughters of Philip that Barsabas, who was also entitled to the name Justus, was forced by unbelievers to drink the poison of a snake but in the name of Christ was preserved from harm. He relates also other marvels, in particular the resurrection of the mother of Manaemus from the dead. Concerning those who were raised by Christ from the dead he relates that they survived to the time of Hadrian.

---

language closer to what Eusebius (*Chronicon*, ed. Helm [1956], 182-183, 404) had to say about James the Just than what Acts 12:2 has to say about James the apostle (J. H. Bernard, *Commentary on John* [New York, 1929], I, xxxviii-xlii). Bernard further hazards the suggestion that the reference to the "second treatise" here had something to do with the second "treatise" of Eusebius' ecclesiastical history in which the story of James's martyrdom is found (*H.E.* 2.23.20). Note that the epitome is headed by the words: "A collection of different narratives from the birth of our Lord according to the flesh, and onwards, beginning with the first book of the Ecclesiastical History of Eusebius Pamphili." John, as well as James, is mentioned perhaps through some confusion with John the Baptist (Zahn, *Introduction*, III, 205-206); or under the influence of the tradition preserved in the Syriac calendar from the fifth century, which commemorates John and James together as martyrs on December 27 (W. Lockton, *Theology*, 5 [1922], 83).

The account of the two miracles parallels closely Eusebius, *H.E.* 3.39.9. The additional features ("poison of a snake"—see Mark 16:18; "the mother of Manaemus"—probably the Manaen of Acts 13:1 [for the name see Josephus, *Ant.* 9.229, 232]) are hardly impressive enough to prove independent acquaintance with Papias; they may represent contamination from other legendary materials. In any event, it is clear that the last line of the fragment attributes to Papias what in fact Quadratus says about those raised by Jesus, as reported by Eusebius, *H.E.* 4.3.2, a few pages after his account of Papias (and the epitomizer misunderstood Quadratus' expression "our own times" to refer to "the time of Hadrian"). It is likely, then, that the difference between Eusebius, *H.E.* 3.39.9 and the epitome as to just what miracle was handed on by Philip's daughters is just another such confusion. If the epitomizer or his source can so mix up (notes taken on?) Papias and Quadratus, the possibility that he also confuses

XII. The martyrdom of John (George the Sinner, *Chronicon*, Codex Coislinianus 305; H. Nolte, *Theologische Quartalschrift*, 44 [1862], 466; cf. *PG*, CX, 19)

1. After Domitian, Nerva reigned a year. He recalled John from the island and left him free to settle in Ephesus. At that time he was the only survivor of the twelve disciples, and after writing the Gospel named after him was honored by martyrdom. 2. For Papias, the bishop of Hierapolis, who had seen him with his own eyes, asserts in the second treatise of the *Dominical Oracles* that he was slain by the Jews—thus clearly bringing to fulfillment together with his brother the prediction of Christ regarding them and their own confession and resolve regarding this matter. For when the Lord had said to them: "Are you able to

---

(notes taken on?) *H.E.* 2.23.20 and Papias ("James" slain by the Jews) is strengthed. Note that Photius (*Bibliothecae Codices* 35; *PG*, CIII, 68) had no high regard for Philip of Side's ability.

In short, our author appears to be dependent primarily on Eusebius' account of Papias and to have enriched what interested him there with fragments from other sources. He is a bungler and cannot be trusted. (Naturally it is impossible to use the reference to Hadrian's time in dating Papias' work.)

All MSS of George's *Chronicon* (ninth century) except Coislinianus 305 have "John the theologian" (the Evangelist) go "to his rest in peace." The composer of the exceptional MS, whose text we translate, seems to have gone out of his way to collect references concerning John's end. In (1) he follows the opening sentences found in all the other MSS, changing "went to his rest in peace" to "was honored by martyrdom." In (2) the reason for the change becomes clear: our author has information from Papias and has reflected on Mark 10:38-39. In (3) he makes reference to Origen's remarks on Mark 10:35-40 in his *Commentary on Matthew* 16.6 (ed. Klostermann, I, 486). This is followed by a quotation from Eusebius, *H.E.* 3.1.1, which is to be found also in the other MSS.

Our author is uncritical. Section 2 has to do with a *martyr's death*; whereas Origen sees the fulfillment of the prophecy of Mark 10:35-40 in James's martyrdom and *John's later exile to Patmos!* Moreover, the quotation from Eusebius hardly adds, as our author implies, evidence of John's martyrdom. Especially the appearance of the unusual title "Dominical Oracles" for Papias' work (along with the term *logos* for the individual books) in both this and the preceding fragment suggests that they go back to a common source or that George was directly dependent on the epitomizer (de Boor, *TU*, V, 178). In either event it seems clear that the form in which this information came to our

drink the cup which I drink" and they had eagerly assented and agreed, he said: "You will drink my cup and will be baptized with the baptism with which I am baptized" [Mark 10:38-39]. Such is what one would expect; for God cannot lie. 3. The learned Origen also confirms this account in his interpretation of the Gospel According to Matthew [16.6], intimating that he knew from the successors of the apostles that John had suffered martyrdom. Furthermore, the well-informed Eusebius says in his *Ecclesiastical History*: "Thomas was allotted Parthia, but John, Asia; he stayed there and died in Ephesus" [Eusebius, *H.E.* 3.1].

XIII. The Gospel of John (Codex Vaticanus Alexandrinus 14; J. B. Pitra, *Analecta Sacra*, II [1884], 160)

1. The Gospel of John was revealed and given to the churches by John when he was yet in the flesh as a man of Hierapolis by

---

author was so bald as to enable him to link it with the usual traditions about John with no sense of embarrassment. To be sure, he has not given us all that his source contained; his reference to James is oblique (no doubt because of his interest in John here); but it is unlikely that any really significant information has been omitted. The interpolator certainly knew nothing to cause him to suspect that the tradition regarding the martyrdom of James and John implied an early date for the death of the latter and the impossibility of a stay in Ephesus to an old age.

This is one of the "anti-Marcionite prologues" reconstructed by D. de Bruyne, *Revue Bénédictine*, 40 (1928), 193-214. The reliability of the passage is somewhat enhanced in this account of the matter. Unfortunately, as E. Gutwenger has shown (*ThS*, 7 [1946], 393-409), the whole theory is weaker than is often realized and the prologue must stand on its own rather fragile feet. Its clumsy Latin suggests a Greek original; some of the Latin phraseology (*adhuc in corpore constituto* and *contraria sentiebat*) is characteristic of fourth-century writers.

It is clearly anti-Marcionite and seems particularly concerned to insist on Johannine authorship for the Fourth Gospel. It is possible that this is directed primarily against the Marcionite Adamantius (*Dialogue* 2.12) from *ca.* A.D. 300, since there is no record of any special attack by Marcion himself on the Fourth Gospel. This suggestion (of Gutwenger) assumes that the prologue ought to be taken as a unity.

Reasons for treating section 2 as a later addition revolve about the impossibility of such a confrontation between John and Marcion. The

the name of Papias, a dear disciple of John, has recorded in his exoteric—that is, at the end of his five books. 2. Indeed, he wrote down the Gospel, as John dictated, correctly. But Marcion the

---

attempt to isolate and eliminate this element usually represents a conservative effort to save as much of the prologue as possible; at the same time it is to be noted (a) that some conservative scholars try to save the prologue as a whole by critical operations with the text, and (b) that others who do not accept the claims of the prologue nevertheless have contributed suggestions that give it greater coherence and credibility.

Section 2 would be less clumsy if with Bacon pp. 459-461 we put a full stop after *dictante Iohanne* and begin the next sentence with *recte vero*. More important difficulties are eliminated by Annand (*SJT*, 9 [1956], 59-60), who puts a full stop after *abiectus est* and joins *a Iohanne* to the next sentence. The result is a rather strange word order, but it makes it possible to understand the confrontation as one between Marcion and Papias. To accomplish the same end, D. de Bruyne had suggested dropping *a Iohanne* or emending it to refer to some Roman church official (for a clever suggestion as to what tradition actually lies behind the statement see Gutwenger, *ThS*, 7 [1946], 407). But such solutions seem unnatural, and it is more likely that we have to do with hazy notions built up on a misunderstanding, say, of Tertullian's language (*Adversus Marcionem* 3.8; *De Praescriptione* 33; *Adversus Praxean* 28; cf. Bacon pp. 457-466). On the untenability of Harnack's suggestion that the tradition originally had to do with a confrontation between Marcion and elders of Asia Minor, see B. W. Bacon, *JTS*, 23 (1922), 134-160.

The idea that Papias was John's amanuensis (so also the proem in the *catena* on John edited by Corderius), is discredited by its link with this anachronism and would, if true, probably have been noted by Eusebius and others before him; it may be modeled on similar relations thought to obtain between apostles and writers of Gospels. Perhaps, as Beyschlag suggests (*TU*, LXXIX, 280, n. 3), the fact that references to *hermēneiai* and to "John" appear close together in Papias' prologue (Eusebius, *H.E.* 3.39.3-4) reminded someone of the passage in which Mark is made Peter's *hermēneutēs* (*H.E.* 3.39.15). Or perhaps "Papias" is a mistake for "Prochorus," the amanuensis of John, according to the Acts of John (Corssen, *ZNW*, 2 [1901], 224). Or perhaps Papias used a verb like *apegrapsā* or *apegraphon* of the authorship of John; it is easy to see how these third-person plurals could have been understood as first-person singulars (Lightfoot, *Essays*, 213-214).

By "documents or letters" the writer understands letters of recommendation. The somewhat uncertain tone of the comment may reflect lack of clarity in his source—e.g., Tertullian, *Adversus Marcionem* 4.3-4 (Bacon pp. 456-457). It seems unlikely that a reference to Mar-

heretic, since he had been disapproved of by him because he held contrary opinions, was rejected by John. To be sure, he had brought documents or letters to him from the brethren who were in Pontus.

---

cion's Bible was originally intended (Gutwenger, *ThS*, 7 [1946], 407).

To return to section 1: "That is, at the end of his" is a gloss to explain the corrupt "exoteric." "Exegetical" probably ought to be read. Annand's suggestion that "exoteric" refers to something on the "wrappings" of Papias' book (or of the Fourth Gospel) seems far-fetched (*SJT*, 9 [1956], 58-59).

It is not perverse, I think, to suggest that sections 1 and 2 stand or fall together. There is nothing to prevent us from regarding both sections as directed against Marcionite criticism of the Fourth Gospel. If this is correct, section 1 is under as dark a cloud as section 2.

By the principles laid down in connection with *H.E.* 3.39.14-17, I think we could expect Eusebius to have quoted Papias on John if he had in fact made any such statements. The elimination of secondary elements must be drastic indeed to reduce the remarks to something which Eusebius would have regarded as unworthy of notice (cf. *H.E.* 5.8.2-4). The same objection may be pressed even more convincingly against those who think that Papias' prologue was originally concerned with Revelation (Bacon pp. 452-455; *HTR*, 23 [1930], 305-307: *manifestatum* refers more naturally to a revelation; Rev. 1:9-11 provides a relevant background for the opening remarks; the Ethiopic subscription to Revelation reads in part, "that vision which he saw in his lifetime") or with Revelation and the Gospel (R. M. Grant, *ATR*, 29 [1947], 172). That Papias actually knew the Gospel of John is believed by many (see p. 105), but that he made any formal statement about it must be doubted. It is not impossible of course that in this case as well as in the case of Revelation, Eusebius was not informed (see p. 114). It is also possible that he suppressed information because he regarded what Papias said as absurd (see p. 114) or because Papias regarded John as verging on Gnosticism (see p. 105). But the internal problems of the text itself suggest that we are dealing with a late tradition which sheds no light on Papias or the Fourth Gospel.

The Traditions of the Elders

We set out here the traditions of the "elders" in Irenaeus, regarded by F. Loofs pp. 311-312 as mediated to him through Papias. In addition to arguments based on details, Loofs presents three general reasons for this view: (1) Irenaeus never suggests that he had personal contact with "the elders"; (2) Irenaeus refers to Papias and his *Exposition* of five books precisely in the context (*Adv. haer.* 5.30-36) where four of these traditions are found—and he regards Papias as "also" having handed on one of them in written form (see on fragment I above); (3) the introductions "the presbyters bear witness" (or "say") seem to be part of the tradition in fragments I and II below and cannot, therefore, be traced to the presbyters themselves.

A similar view of these notices in Irenaeus was already brought forward by Lightfoot (*Essays*, 194-202). In his collection of "the reliquies of the elders" he included also those fragments which spoke of "one better than we are," "the divine elder," "one who was before us," "one of the ancients," "a certain elder," and so forth (J. B. Lightfoot and J. R. Harmer, *The Apostolic Fathers* [London, 1898], 537-562). He recognized, however, that these presuppose "conversations" rather than "published records." Here we are concerned only with traditions of the "elders," for they, if any, appear to be derived from documents. (Of those printed below, fragments VII and VIII from Irenaeus' *Epideixis* are most doubtful in this respect.)

It must be admitted, however, that there are impressive arguments against connecting them with Papias (Zahn, *Forschungen*, VI, 88-94). In any event care must be exercised, since the form that they take may owe much to Irenaeus.

I. The age of Christ (*Adv. haer.* 2.22.5)

[After forty to fifty years a man is said to be moving toward an "advanced age"] which our Lord had when he taught, inasmuch

---

Irenaeus has been discussing the seven ages of man, all of which, he claims, were attained by Christ. This is based on an exegesis of John

as the gospel [John 8:57] and all the elders who lived in Asia with John, the Lord's disciple, testify that John handed down this tradition. For he remained with them until the days of Trajan. Some of them, moreover, saw not only John but also other apostles and heard the same thing from them and testify concerning such an account.

II. Paradise (*Adv. haer.* 5.5.1)

Where then was the first man placed? In paradise clearly, as it is written: "And God planted paradise eastward in Eden, and there he placed the man whom he had formed" [Gen. 2:8]. And from there he was cast forth into this world because of his disobedience [Gen. 3:23-24]. Therefore the elders, disciples of the

---

8:57, the tradition of the elders, and the doctrine of recapitulation. It is directed against the Gnostic chronology of the Gospels. Note that Victorinus, *De Fabr. Mund.* 9, also says that Christ lived out the seven ages of man. Since the latter presents the teaching in a different setting, and since he seems to have (independent?) knowledge of Papias (see p. 92), this idea may go back to the bishop of Hierapolis. Corssen (*ZNW*, 2 [1901], 202-227) even traces to Papias a medieval tradition (in *Codex Bobbiensis* H.150 Inf.) which attributes to Victorinus the following dating of Christ's life: born in A.D. 9, baptized in A.D. 46, crucified in A.D. 58 (see E. von Dobschütz, *TU*, XI, 136-150; cf. D. G. Morin, *JTS*, 7 [1906], 456-459). J. Chapman, however, argues that these dates are the result of later blunders (*JTS*, 8 [1907], 590-606) and that even Irenaeus applied in an overly literal way the "harmless mysticism" of Papias; the latter (like Victorinus) was simply brooding on the number seven without serious regard to chronology (*JTS*, 9 [1908], 42-61; cf. Schwartz, *AkGWG*, 1904, 8). For further remarks on this passage see p. 89.

This fragment speaks of a superterrestrial paradise (see also fragment V below and fragment VII of Papias above). Irenaeus is referring to Enoch and Elijah when he speaks of "those translated." The former in particular was thought to have gone to "paradise" according to Jewish teaching (Jub. 4:23; 1 Enoch 60:8, 23; 70:3-4; cf. 2 Enoch 8:1-8). In *Pesachim* 54a we learn that of the seven things created before the world, one was "the Garden of Eden, as it is written, 'And the Lord planted a Garden [Paradise] in Eden *from aforetime*'" (Gen. 2:8). "From aforetime" is a possible rendering here and probably lies behind the tradition of the elders as well. (Unfortunately the Greek form of Irenaeus' text preserved in the Parallela of John of Damascus omits the scriptural quotation.) This is the type of exegesis found elsewhere in Papias, as we have seen.

apostles, also say that those translated were translated to it—for paradise has been prepared for just men and bearers of the Spirit; to it also Paul the apostle was carried and heard there words unspeakable [2 Cor. 12:4], at least as far as we are concerned in this present life—and those translated shall remain there until the end of all things as inaugurators of incorruptibility.

III. The number 666 (*Adv. haer.* 5.30.1)

[Since the number 666 is found in the best manuscripts of Rev. 13:18] and since those very men who saw the blessed John face to face testify to it and reason teaches us that this number ... of 666 is the number of the name of that beast, I do not know how some have erred [and chosen the number 616 instead].

IV. Creation renewed and liberated (*Adv. haer.* 5.33.3; see fragment I of Papias above)

V. The heavenly rooms (*Adv. haer.* 5.36.1-2)

And as the elders say, then [after the appearance of the new heaven and new earth (Isa. 66:22)] those thought worthy of an abode in heaven will go there, others will enjoy "the delights of paradise" [cf. Ezek. 28:13], others will possess the brightness of

---

This is perhaps the clearest evidence of the use of Revelation by Papias (see fragment V of Papias above). Yet it is not impossible that the elders and Revelation are dependent on a common source as far as the number 666 is concerned; for in other respects there seems to have been some tension between the eschatology of Revelation and that of the elders (see fragment I of Papias above and fragments V and VI below).

See also fragment VII of Papias and fragment II of the elders. The form of the parable to which reference is made is that of Matthew. According to Victorinus (*Commentary on Revelation* 21.1-2) the "city" which comes down at the *beginning* of the millennium (contrast Rev. 20:4–21:2) includes "all that area of the Eastern provinces promised to the patriarch Abraham." In the fragments of the elders this renewed earth probably is thought to continue for all time for those unworthy of paradise or heaven and incapable of further "progressing" toward them (see on fragment I of Papias and fragment VI below).

If the fragment may be connected with Papias, it is the clearest evidence that he used the Gospel of John (14:2)—though the quotation may have been added by Irenaeus. (See also our comments on

the city; for the Savior will be seen everywhere to the degree that those who see him are worthy. And they say that this is the distinction between the dwelling of those bringing forth a hundredfold and those bringing forth sixtyfold and those bringing forth thirtyfold [Matt. 13:8]; the first will be taken up into the heavens, the second will abide in paradise, the third will inhabit the city. And it is for this reason that the Lord said: "In my Father's house are many rooms" [John 14:2].

VI. Steps of salvation (*Adv. haer.* 5.36.2)

The elders, disciples of the apostles, say that this is the order and arrangement of those who are saved and that they advance by such steps and ascend through the Spirit to the Son, through the Son to the Father, the Son finally yielding his task to the Father, as it is also said by the apostle: "For he must reign until he has put all enemies under his feet" [etc., 1 Cor. 15:25].

VII. Faith (*Epid.* 3)

Now it is faith that does this for us, as the elders, the disciples of the apostles, have handed down to us. [There follows the rule of faith.]

VIII. The concord and tranquility of the animals (*Epid.* 61)

As to the union and concord and tranquility of the animals, who are of different kinds and by nature hostile to each other and inimical, the elders say that it will indeed be so at the coming of Christ when he will rule over all.

Eusebius, *H.E.* 3.39.3-4, 14-17.) R. M. Grant (*ATR*, 25 [1943], 220-221) suggests that the form of the quotation (*en tois tou patros mou*, not *en tē oikia tou patros mou*) owes something also to Luke 2:49.

The suggestion here, as in the preceding fragment, is that those who are worthy begin in the millennium to make progress to a higher mode of existence—paradise or heaven.

SELECTED BIBLIOGRAPHY

(Books or articles marked * are cited only by the author's name)

ANNAND, R., "Papias and the Four Gospels," *Scottish Journal of Theology* 9 (1956), 46-62.
*BACON, B. W., *Studies in Matthew*. New York, 1930.
BARTLET, J. V., "Papias's 'Exposition': Its Date and Contents," in *Amicitiae Corolla: A Volume of Essays Presented to James Rendel Harris*, ed. H. G. Wood (London, 1933), 15-44.
BARTLET, V., "Papias," in J. Hastings (ed.), *A Dictionary of Christ and the Gospels*, II, 309-312. New York, 1912.
BAUER, W., *Rechtgläubigkeit und Ketzerei im ältesten Christentum* (*Beiträge zur historischen Theologie*, Vol. X). Tübingen, 1934.
BEYSCHLAG, K., "Herkunft und Eigenart der Papiasfragmente," in *Studia Patristica IV*, *Texte und Untersuchungen* 79 (1961), 268-280.
BOOR, C. DE, *Neue Fragmente des Papias, Hegesippus und Pierius*, *Texte und Untersuchungen*, 5, Leipzig, 1888.
CHAPMAN, J., "On an Apostolic Tradition that Christ Was Baptized in 46 and Crucified Under Nero," *Journal of Theological Studies* 8 (1907), 590-606.
——, "Papias on the Age of Our Lord," *Journal of Theological Studies* 9 (1908), 42-61.
——, *John the Presbyter and the Fourth Gospel*. Oxford, 1911.
COLSON, F. H., "*Taxei* in Papias," *Journal of Theological Studies* 14 (1913), 62-69.
DOBSCHÜTZ, E. VON, *Das Kerygma Petri*, *Texte und Untersuchungen*, 11, Leipzig, 1893.
DONOVAN, J., *The Logia in Ancient and Recent Literature*. Cambridge, Eng., 1924.
FINDLAY, J. A., "The First Gospel and the Book of Testimonies," in *Amicitiae Corolla: A Volume of Essays Presented to James Rendel Harris*, ed. H. G. Wood (London, 1933), 57-71.
GÄCHTER, P., "Die Dolmetscher der Apostel," *Zeitschrift für katholische Theologie* 60 (1936), 161-187.
GRANT, R. M., "The Oldest Gospel Prologues," *Anglican Theological Review* 23 (1941), 231-245.
GRY, L., "Le Papias des belles promesses messianiques," *Vivre et Penser* 3 (1944), 112-124.
——, "Hénoch X,19 et les belles promesses de Papias," *Revue Biblique* 53 (1946), 197-206.

GUSTAFSSON, B., "Eusebius' Principles in Handling His Sources, as Found in His Church History, Books I-VII," in *Studia Patristica IV, Texte und Untersuchungen* 79 (1961), 429-441.
GUTWENGER, E., "The Anti-Marcionite Prologues," *Theological Studies* 7 (1946), 393-409.
———, "Papias: eine chronologische Studie," *Zeitschrift für katholische Theologie* 69 (1947), 385-416.
HATCH, W. H. P., "Ueber den Namen Papias," *Zeitschrift für die neutestamentliche Wissenschaft* 12 (1911), 83.
HAUSLEITER, J. (ed.), *Victorini Episcopi Petavionensis Opera (Corpus Scriptorum Ecclesiasticorum Latinorum*, Vol. XXXXIX). Vienna, 1916.
HELM, R., *Eusebius Werke*, Vol. VII: *Die Chronik des Hieronymus (Die griechischen christlichen Schriftsteller der ersten drei Jahrhunderte)*. Berlin, 2d ed., 1956.
*HOMMES, N. J., *Het Testimoniaboek: Studien over O.T. Citaten in het N.T. en bij de Patres, met critische Beschouwingen over de Theorieen van J. Rendel Harris en D. Plooy*. Amsterdam, 1935.
KLEIST, J. A., *Rereading the Papias Fragment on St. Mark (Saint Louis University Studies: Series A: Humanities*, Vol. I/1). St. Louis, 1945.
KÜRZINGER, J., "Das Papiaszeugnis und die Erstgestalt des Matthäusevangeliums," *Biblische Zeitschrift*, N.F. 4 (1960), 19-38.
*LAMPE, G. W. H. (ed.), *A Patristic Greek Lexicon*. Oxford, 1961-.
LAWLOR, H. J., "Eusebius on Papias," *Hermathena* 43 (1922), 167-222.
*———, and OULTON, J. E. L., *Eusebius, Bishop of Caesarea: The Ecclesiastical History and the Martyrs of Palestine*. 2 vols. London, 1954.
LIGHTFOOT, J. B., *Essays on the Work Entitled Supernatural Religion*. London, 1889.
LOCKTON, W., "The Martyrdom of John," *Theology* 5 (1922), 80-83.
*LOOFS, F., *Theophilus von Antiochien Adversus Marcionem und die anderen theologischen Quellen bei Irenaeus, Texte und Untersuchungen* 46, Leipzig, 1930.
MULLINS, T. Y., "Papias on Mark's Gospel," *Vigiliae Christianae* 14 (1960), 216-224.
MUNCK, J., "Presbyters and Disciples of the Lord in Papias," *Harvard Theological Review* 52 (1959), 223-243.
SCHWARTZ, E., *Ueber den Tod der Söhne Zebedaei: ein Beitrag zur Geschichte des Johannesevangelium (Abhandlungen der königlichen Gesellschaft der Wissenschaften zu Göttingen: Philologisch-historische Klasse*, N.F. Vol. VII/5). Berlin, 1904. (Abbreviation: AkGWG, 1904.)
TAYLOR, R. O. P., *The Groundwork of the Gospels*. Oxford, 1946.
WALZ, C. (ed.), *Rhetores Graeci*. 9 vols. Stuttgart-Tübingen, 1832-1836.

WRIGHT, A., "Taxei in Papias," *Journal of Theological Studies* 14 (1913), 298-300.
ZAHN, TH., *Forschungen zur Geschichte des neutestamentlichen Kanons*, Vol. VI: *I. Apostle und Apostelschüler in der Provinz Asien. II. Brüder und Vettern Jesu.* Leipzig, 1900.
──, *Introduction to the New Testament*. 3 vols. New York, 1909.

www.ingramcontent.com/pod-product-compliance
Lightning Source LLC
Chambersburg PA
CBHW050829160426
43192CB00010B/1954